SUPPORTING KIDS AND TEENS WITH EXAM STRESS IN SCHOOL

by the same author

Helping Kids and Teens with ADHD in School
A Workbook for Classroom Support and Managing Transitions
Joanne Steer and Kate Horstmann
Illustrated by Jason Edwards
ISBN 978 1 84310 663 0
eISBN 978 1 84642 923 1

of related interest

The Mental Health and Wellbeing Workout for Teens (forthcoming)
Skills and Exercises from ACT and CBT for Healthy Thinking
Paula Nagel
Illustrated by Gary Bainbridge
ISBN 978 1 78592 394 4
eISBN 978 1 78450 753 4

My Anxiety Handbook
Getting Back on Track
Sue Knowles, Bridie Gallagher and Phoebe McEwen
Illustrated by Emmeline Pidgen
ISBN 978 1 78592 440 8
eISBN 978 1 78450 813 5

Starving the Exam Stress Gremlin
A Cognitive Behavioural Therapy Workbook on Managing Exam Stress for Young People
Kate Collins-Donnelly
ISBN 978 1 84905 698 4
eISBN 978 1 78450 214 0

The Healthy Coping Colouring Book and Journal
Creative Activities to Help Manage Stress, Anxiety and Other Big Feelings
Pooky Knightsmith
Illustrated by Emily Hamilton
ISBN 978 1 78592 139 1
eISBN 978 1 78450 405 2

Starving the Anxiety Gremlin
A Cognitive Behavioural Therapy Workbook on Anxiety Management for Young People
Kate Collins-Donnelly
ISBN 978 1 84905 341 9
eISBN 978 0 85700 673 8

SUPPORTING KIDS AND TEENS WITH EXAM STRESS IN SCHOOL

A WORKBOOK

JOANNE STEER

Illustrations by **Suzy Ross**

Jessica Kingsley *Publishers*
London and Philadelphia

First published in 2019
by Jessica Kingsley Publishers
73 Collier Street
London N1 9BE, UK
and
400 Market Street, Suite 400
Philadelphia, PA 19106, USA

www.jkp.com

Copyright © Joanne Steer 2019
Illustrations copyright © Suzy Ross 2019

Library of Congress Cataloging in Publication Data
A CIP catalog record for this book is available from the Library of Congress

British Library Cataloguing in Publication Data
A CIP catalogue record for this book is available from the British Library

ISBN 978 1 78592 467 5
eISBN 978 1 78450 851 7

Printed and bound by CPI Group (UK) Ltd, Croydon, CR0 4YY

Acknowledgements

From Jo:

I would like to thank my husband James and my three children Neave, Xavier and Adeline for their patience and support during the writing of this book. I hope you all forgive me for the Sundays I spent in the office working on this! I would like to thank Suzy for her fantastic illustrations, her attention to detail and her enthusiasm. Who would have thought the school playground could lead to this project? Thank you also to my Mum, Sarah Head and my editor Amy Lankester-Owen for their advice and editing of previous versions. Finally, a thank you to Kate, who started this journey of authorship with me over ten years ago when we wrote our first book. I would never have been brave enough to do this without our joint adventure the first time around!

From Suzy:

I would like to extend a massive thank you to Jo. This has been an amazing opportunity for me and I owe it all to you, so thank you very much. Not only has it been wonderful to have my first opportunity to see my illustrations published in a book through a publisher, but it has also meant so much to be involved in a project to do with exam stress. This is something I have struggled with myself over the years, both at school and beyond.

I would also like to thank my fabulous husband David for giving me the push and support I needed to work for my dream of being an illustrator. Without you, I wouldn't have even contemplated putting myself out there and trying.

Contents

CHAPTER 1

Welcome

An Introduction for Adults

Hello and welcome to my new workbook! I am so pleased that you have decided to pick up this book and look inside. This workbook is similar in style to my previous book, *Helping Kids and Teens with ADHD in School*, but this time I am focusing on exam stress. I know from personal and professional experience just how stressful exams can be, but this book aims to help with this stress. I hope that by sharing information, knowledge and strategies I can make a real difference to the lives of young people at these challenging times. The ideas in this workbook are ones I have used and developed in my work as a clinical psychologist over the last 14 years.

I anticipate that this workbook is most suited for use with children and young people between the ages of 10 and 16 years. It is designed with a broad range of individuals in mind, including teachers, teaching support staff, therapists, psychologists and parents.

This book is written from the following underlying principles:

- Acknowledging the individuality of young people and promoting their development of positive self-worth underpins their success.

- Building relationships is crucial – young people can easily feel isolated and withdraw from those around them at times of challenge.

- Recognising and understanding a problem is one of the biggest steps in making a real difference.

- Knowledge and understanding should be shared with the young person in a way that makes sense to them, giving them the ownership and insight required for change.

- Young people need to be involved in all steps of the process (learning, implementing and evaluating) in order to ensure that lasting change can be made.

- Small changes can make a *huge* difference to the lives of young people – choose only a few strategies at a time and do them well.

- Strategies are only effective if they are tailored to the individual, introduced in a way that is consistent, and then evaluated and tweaked.

- To work towards independence, skills and coping strategies need to be taught in a planned and gradual manner with tangible assistance and support.

- Adults need to meet the young person half way by making changes to their own expectations and behaviours.

- Having *fun* is essential when engaging and motivating young people.

It is important to acknowledge that this book is not driven by specific research. It utilises theory and strategies from a variety of fields and draws heavily on clinical experience.

HOW TO USE THIS BOOK

There are ten chapters and each one is divided into sections that should help you to navigate and plan. All pages marked ⚓ may be photocopied or downloaded at www.jkp.com/voucher using the code NOYXOMY. Each page and worksheet is labelled as one of the following areas.

Introducing

Key purpose: These pages provide insights and perspectives on the topic and how it relates to young people experiencing exam stress. They are designed more for adults than young people, though you'll notice that this section in Chapter 2 is written as an introduction for the young person, and is designed to be read with an adult. 'Introducing' sections also provide outlines of the broad objectives for each chapter.

User tips: Read through this section before starting work on a chapter, so that you can plan how to discuss and explore the topic with the young person.

Detect and Reflect

Key purpose: 'Detect and Reflect' worksheets encourage the young person to think about the topic, their individual skills in this area and how other people around them think about this issue. 'Detect and Reflect' attempts to broaden perspectives on issues in order to normalise experiences, and lays the foundation for problem solving and goal setting.

User tips: The worksheets have been ordered in such a way that they build on a concept, but you can complete them in any order you like. Discussions around these worksheets don't have to take place sitting down at a table – you can have them while doing an activity such as kicking a ball around, doing some cooking or even bouncing on a trampoline!

Give It A Go

Key purpose: 'Give It A Go' worksheets ask the young person to trial a range of strategies as well as solve problems. There is often an element of evaluating and rating the effectiveness of strategies and their potential for use in everyday life.

User tips: Some of the activities require more preparation and completion time than others so forward planning is required. Most tasks don't need to be completed in the set order; however, it is always good to have done the 'Detect and Reflect' worksheets first to give perspective. Remember that this is the fun part of each chapter so try to make sure it's enjoyable! Try these challenges out for yourself and get involved. Make sure you spend time reflecting and evaluating your efforts!

↝ Pulling It Together

Key purpose: 'Pulling It Together' worksheets are designed to encourage problem solving in 'real-life' situations to identify key points of learning from the chapter and help you decide if further work is needed. This is really important for the planning and goal-setting phase that is mapped out in the final chapter.

User tips: Go back through all the worksheets in the chapter and together reflect on what has been discovered so that there is an integrated picture of needs and priorities. If there is a disagreement as to areas of concern and focus, try to acknowledge everyone's opinion in writing.

✓ Top Tips

Key purpose: 'Top Tips' are divided into separate sheets for young people and adults. They provide additional information, practical considerations and guidance on implementation.

User tips: It is recommended that you read these before starting each chapter as they contain extra information that might be helpful in guiding you and the young person. They can be particularly helpful when working on developing specific goals or strategies. Some tip sheets have been designed for use as information sheets to help educate others.

☆ Resources

Key purpose: These lists of additional resources have been added as they may help guide further exploration of support in a particular area.

User tips: These lists are *not* exhaustive – there are lots of other great resources around and always more being developed! Make sure you research any products first in order to check if they will meet your specific needs.

HOW TO CREATE LEARNING SESSIONS
General hints

- Adult support may need to be provided for the completion of worksheets, and reflection on their content, in order to ensure learning and best determine effective strategies.

- Photocopy or download worksheets and create a folder – one for the adults and one for the young person. The young person may wish to take their folder home between sessions or leave it with the adult until the final session.

- Balance 'Detect and Reflect' worksheets with 'Give It A Go' so there is a mix of practical and thinking activities.

- Use multiple methods to complete worksheets – scribing (e.g. you write while having a discussion with the young person), using pictures or typing onto a laptop or tablet.

- Photocopy or download the 'Reflections' form at the end of this chapter in 'Top Tips'. At the end of each session, quickly make a note of your thoughts.

- Photocopy or download the 'My To Do List' form at the end of the chapter and use this with the young person to set homework tasks and as a prompt sheet on what to bring to the next session.

- Be creative and add your own touches and interests to the sessions!

- You can change the order of the chapters to some degree. However, ensure 'Welcome' and 'Getting Started' are completed first.

Group sessions

Groups can be an effective way of teaching the skills from this book. They can also provide additional motivation and promote shared learning and problem solving. There are many possible formats and settings in which you could run groups from this workbook, including general provision for all students on exam stress, targeted groups at school, and community groups set up through voluntary or mental health services. It is recommended that you:

- consider the ratio of staff to young people; keep the group to around eight or ten if you are targeting young people with specific anxiety needs

- use motivating and positive reward systems for effort and contribution rather than attainment

- complete some of the 'Detect and Reflect' worksheets as a group to create variety and facilitate discussion; use a whiteboard or flipchart to provide visual support

- set some worksheets as takeaway activities to be completed at home between sessions

- utilise strategies you have learned within the sessions, such as exercise, mindfulness exercises and relaxation

- provide a break to ensure time for the young people to socialise and make connections outside the formal activities.

TURNING STRATEGIES INTO ACTION

The final chapter recommends a process for implementing strategies in a way that includes the young person as a partner in working towards simple and achievable goals. It is up to you to decide whether goals are agreed and worked on at the same time as you continue to work through this book (e.g. strategies from 'Looking After Yourself' are implemented while also working through the remaining chapters). Alternatively, you can complete the entire workbook before goals and strategies are selected. This decision will depend on a variety of factors including your available resources and the timing of forthcoming exams.

GETTING STARTED FOR ADULTS

The next few worksheets are for *you*! They will take you through some important reflections and activities that will help to guide your own learning during this process. The adults around the young person – the parents, teachers and support staff – are often *the most powerful* influences on determining positive outcomes. So the more that we can all learn about managing exam stress and establish helpful habits, while reflecting on our own beliefs and actions, the better their future will be.

You have just finished Chapter 1, 'Introducing' and now it's over to you to try to 'Detect and Reflect' and then 'Give It A Go'. Finish off with 'Pulling It Together', some 'Top Tips' and 'Resources' and a relaxing cup of tea or coffee – you will have earned it!

The Big Issues

What are your young person's main strengths?

From your perspective, what are the main concerns for your young person?

How would you rate your knowledge of stress or anxiety, how it impacts on young people and how to provide support?

List strategies or adaptations that you already know are effective in supporting the young person. Are these used consistently?

We All Worry

We all experience worry regularly in our lives. Throughout our lifetime we develop our own coping strategies to manage these feelings. It is useful to think about our own worries as adults and the coping strategies we use to help us better understand the young people we work with. Consider the following questions to increase your self-awareness:

What did you worry most about as a child or teenager? How did you cope with this worry? Did you get stressed about it and stop doing something because of it?

_____

_____

_____

_____

_____

Did you ever find yourself experiencing exam stress as a young person or adult? How did you manage this?

_____

_____

_____

_____

_____

As an adult, how do you manage stress in your life? Try and consider both unsuccessful and successful strategies.

_____

_____

_____

_____

_____

How do you feel when you have to go for a job interview, give a presentation or do something you are unfamiliar with? What kind of thoughts go through your head at these times?

_____

_____

_____

_____

Compare your answers with those of your friends, family or colleagues. You might be surprised at what you find!

Always Put Your Own Oxygen Mask On First

You probably know that on an aeroplane flight you are advised in the event of a crash to always put your own oxygen mask on first before your child's. The same rule applies when you are supporting a young person with exam stress, whether you are their parent, teacher or therapist. In order to support them in the best way possible, you need to make sure you are looking after yourself, your own emotional wellbeing and anxieties. Perhaps as you work through this book you may discover some strategies that you can try out yourself. Use this page to review your own self-care and what areas you may wish to improve on.

Strategy	Never	Occasionally	Often	Always
Drink plenty of water				
Eat a balanced diet				
Get a good night's sleep				
Exercise regularly				
Enjoy hobbies				
Practise relaxation				
Practise mindfulness exercises				

Considering the table above, which one or two areas will you aim to improve over the next few weeks? Write your goal(s) below.

_____

_____

_____

_____

_____

Welcome

Look back through the worksheets you have completed to help answer the questions below.

What three things can you congratulate yourself on for already knowing/doing?

1. _____

_____

2. _____

_____

3. _____

_____

What three new points of learning or reflection can you list?

1. _____

_____

2. _____

_____

3. _____

_____

My To Do List

Tasks to do at home:

Date given:	Tasks:	Date due:

Things to bring to the next session: (use a checklist for packing your bag)

1. Tasks completed at home (see list above) ☐

Next session

Day and date	Time	Venue

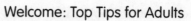

Reflections

Chapter _____

Points of learning for young person:	Points of learning for me:
Things to explore/follow up on/research:	Things with potential to work well:
Strengths/positives:	Things to share with other people:

Other observations/issues:

Five Things Everyone Needs to Know about Helping Young People with Exam Stress

1. Understanding is the key

- Learn about exam stress and anxiety and how they impact on the young person and their life from their point of view.

- Remember to always consider the *why* behind their actions – their difficulties are genuine.

- Strive to educate others and share positive stories and solutions.

2. Teach skills

- Provide a supportive and positive environment for the practice and learning of skills.

- Help develop skills to maximise calmness, identify and respond to stress and develop a healthy lifestyle.

3. Make the young person an active partner

- Discuss individual strengths and difficulties in an open, positive and constructive way.

- Involve them in making decisions, implementing strategies and evaluation.

- Link things to their own goals and priorities – make it meaningful and motivating!

4. Positive role models

- Try to ensure that adults supporting the young person are positive role models in managing stress and anxiety in their own lives.

- Where possible, openly share stressful situations that have been dealt with in the past and what you have learned from these.

5. Consider changes to the system

- The strategies used to support young people with exam stress are great for all individuals.

- These principles have been successfully adopted in schools, classrooms and families.

WELCOME: RESOURCES
Books

- *Can I tell you about Anxiety?: A guide for friends, family and professionals* by Lucy Willetts and Polly Waite, illustrated by Kaiyee Tay, 2014, Jessica Kingsley Publishers.

- *Overcoming Your Child's Fears and Worries: A self-help guide using Cognitive Behavioural Techniques* by Cathy Cresswell and Lucy Willetts, 2007, Robinson.

- *Helping Your Anxious Child: A Step-by-Step Guide for Parents* by Ronald Rapee, 2009, New Harbinger.

- *Helping Your Anxious Teen: Positive Parenting Strategies to Help Your Teen Beat Fear, Stress, and Worry* by Sheila Achar Josephs, 2017, New Harbinger.

Websites

- www.anxietyuk.org.uk

- www.anxietybc.com/parenting/parent-child

- www.youngminds.org.uk

CHAPTER 2

Getting Started

WHAT YOU NEED TO KNOW

This workbook is written and designed for young people experiencing exam stress – people just like you. I hope that it will help you discover and practise different ideas that can help you at home and school. This book can be used at any time; I know that exams and tests happen all year round!

This book might be a little different from some others that you have seen. I have worked with lots of young people with exam stress, and they have helped me understand a few things, such as:

- You already know a lot of stuff about yourself, like some of the things that work well for you and some of the things that don't.

- The people close to you at home and school also have lots of great information about you and your skills.

- Teamwork between you and the people helping you is important – you all need to be involved in making decisions, plans, changing things and trying them out.

- Changes don't just happen overnight – things need to be researched, tested and perfected. This is no different from designing, producing and marketing a new app.

- It's good to have fun while you are learning!

Each chapter in this book has a specific topic to work through. Within each chapter, there are different types of worksheets for you to complete; some of these ask you to survey people you know, others ask you to draw or write about your experiences and some will give you special tasks to try out.

There are three young people who will work with you and keep you entertained throughout the book. Here's your chance to meet them:

Hi! I'm Oliver. I am 10 years old and my favourite things are probably football and computer games. I spend my weekends playing football, watching football and playing football on the computer! I will soon be doing my SATs exams at school. *Everyone* keeps going on about how important they are: my parents, my grandparents and my teacher. All this talk about the exams is making me feel worried and stressed.

Hello, my name is Lily. I am 16 years old and I like hanging out with my friends, and when I am not hanging out with them I am chatting to them on my phone. At school, my favourite subjects are English and history and I am really hoping to go to university and study one of these. I have always worried about exams but over the last year I have become really stressed out preparing for my GCSEs. In my mocks I felt so sick and dizzy I thought I was going to have to leave the room. I really want to do well but am finding it hard to focus as I am so worried.

I am Aiden and I am 14 years old and I have autism spectrum condition (ASC). I am a bit different from other people my age, but you wouldn't know it from looking at me. ASC means that I think in a different way from others and sometimes find friendships and getting on with other people difficult. I find school quite stressful a lot of the time, but do enjoy maths, which I am really good at. I have a dog called Rubik who I like to play with at home; he helps me feel calm sometimes. I also have a good friend Amir who comes over to my house and we play on the console together. I am starting to think about my GCSEs and have done some end-of-year exams at school, which I found really tough.

A good tip from Lily:

Photocopy or download the worksheets from this book and then put them in a folder to make your own 'book'. You could buy a special folder and decorate it. The adult you are working with might also need their own folder.

Have fun getting started!

All About Me

Fill in the pyramid below to create a profile of you as a unique person; you could write or draw your answers. What things do you like eating or doing? What is your personality like? What don't you like doing? What are your top five films, computer games, books or songs?

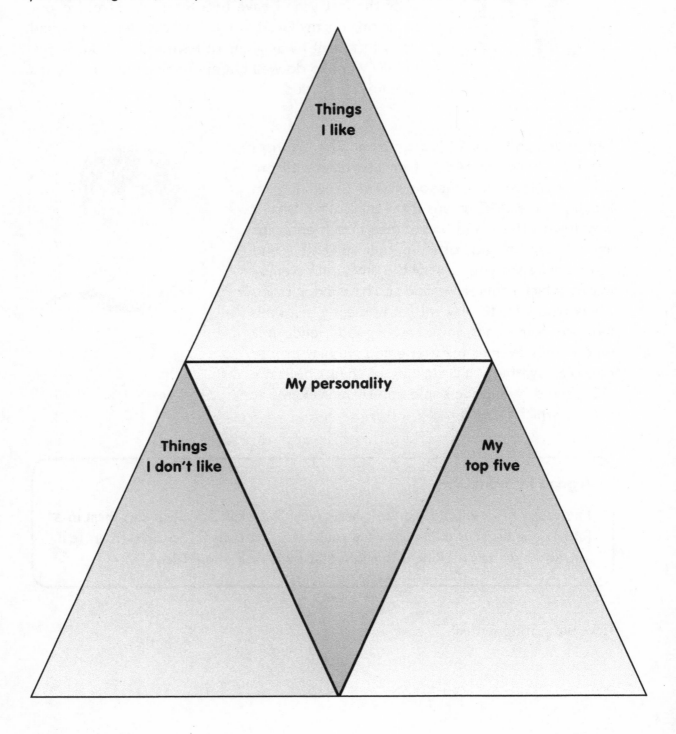

What is Anxiety/Stress?

What do you think stress is? Complete the mind map below by writing about or drawing what the word stress means to you.

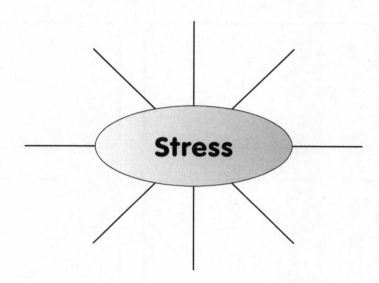

STRESS SYMPTOMS

These are some symptoms to look out for which probably mean you are stressed. Tick any that you are experiencing.

Poor appetite	☐	Aches and pains with no cause	☐
Increased heart rate	☐	Loss of interest in your hobbies	☐
Constant tiredness	☐	More grumpy or snappy than usual	☐
Problems falling asleep	☐	Feeling dizzy	☐
Headaches	☐	Forgetfulness	☐

Identifying Stress for You

Think about a typical day (maybe yesterday) and complete the worksheet below to help you work out what are the things that make you stressed or anxious. Don't worry if none of these are to do with exams or tests!

When?	What is stressing me?	How does it make me feel?
Before school		
At school		
After school		
In the evening		

What the Others Say

Everyone with exam stress is different! Yet some of the ways that exam stress makes you feel and how it affects your life might be similar to what other young people go through. Read these quotes from Oliver, Lily and Aiden about their exam stress and use a highlighter to mark any bits that are similar to the way you have felt.

Oliver: I used to like going to school, I played football with my friends before we went in to class, at break and at lunch, and my teacher is kind and fun. Lately, I wake up and don't really want to go in to school, my tummy hurts a lot. We have been practising for our Year 6 SATs, doing previous test papers. I have found them quite hard and I am worried about the real ones. I don't feel like playing football as much at the moment. Mum says she thinks I am stressed about the exams.

Lily: I have been taking tests and exams for a long time and managed okay in the past. I always study really hard for my exams. In the evenings and weekends I am in my room revising. I even listen to podcasts on my phone when I am getting the bus to school and back. I seem to spend all my spare time revising, but I know it will be worth it if I get good results! Recently, I have found revising really difficult. I keep losing my concentration or forget what I learned the day before. I am really worried that I might mess up my GCSEs and then I won't get to study the A-levels I want or go to university. I have been feeling sick and dizzy quite a lot and I keep bursting out crying. I think I am really getting stressed out about these exams.

Aiden: School is a stressful place to be for me and exams make it even worse! I find it really hard sitting in a quiet room with all the other kids from my year. I can't concentrate on the questions as all the sounds, sights and smells around me fill my mind; it could be the smell of someone's mint sweets, the sound of someone clicking their pen or tapping their foot, or the teachers walking up and down. I am so busy thinking about all this and then I realise I've only written two sentences and 20 minutes have gone. My teacher has said I might be able to work in a smaller room next time. I hope so or I will never finish all the questions!

Understanding Your Exam Stress

In order to help us manage our exam stress better, it is important to understand it and how it affects us. Oliver has completed the shapes below to help him understand his worry about his Year 6 SATs better.

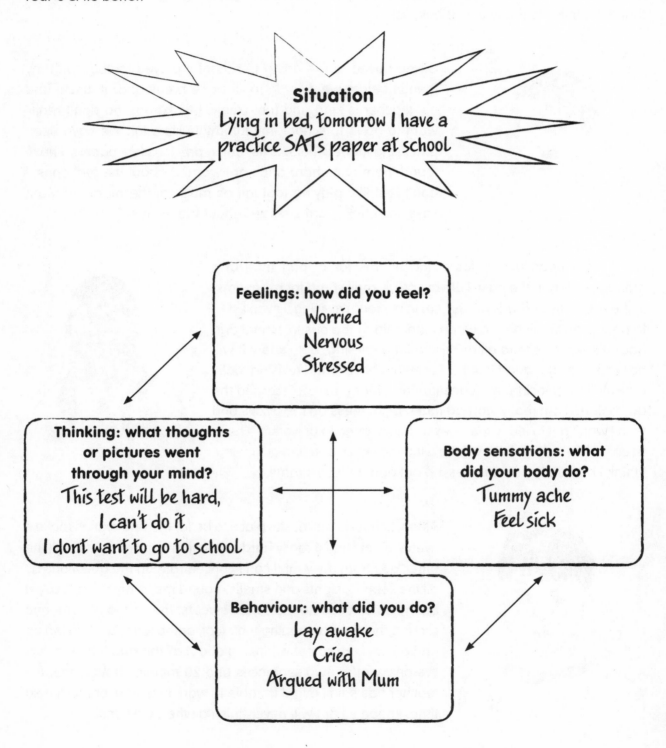

Situation
Lying in bed, tomorrow I have a practice SATs paper at school

Feelings: how did you feel?
Worried
Nervous
Stressed

Thinking: what thoughts or pictures went through your mind?
This test will be hard, I can't do it
I dont want to go to school

Body sensations: what did your body do?
Tummy ache
Feel sick

Behaviour: what did you do?
Lay awake
Cried
Argued with Mum

Understanding Your Exam Stress

Think about a time you have recently felt stressed or worried, perhaps about a test you were going to take, how much revision you had to do or after an argument with your parents. Complete the shapes below to help you better understand your stress and how it affects you.

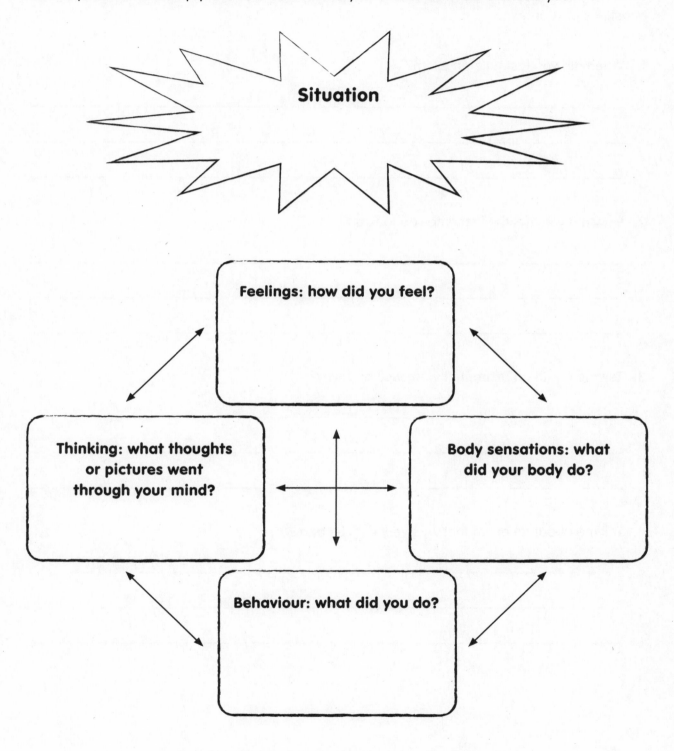

Exam Stress: A Trip Down Memory Lane

This worksheet will help you to find out what someone else remembers about exam stress. Ask a parent, carer, relative, teacher or neighbour if you can interview them. You want to ask about what it was like for them when they took exams, so use the questions below or make up some questions of your own.

1. When did you first take an exam?

    _____

    _____

    _____

2. How did you feel the first time you took an exam?

    _____

    _____

    _____

3. Tell me about an exam that went well and why?

    _____

    _____

    _____

4. Tell me about an exam that was very difficult and why?

    _____

    _____

    _____

5. Do you have any top tips for taking exams?

_____

_____

_____

6. Have you had to do any exams as an adult? How did they go?

_____

_____

_____

7. Tell me about something embarrassing or silly that happened during an exam.

_____

_____

_____

Add questions of your own below.

_____

_____

_____

_____

You Are Not Alone!

Have a look at these websites or any books can you find on exam stress:

- www.youngminds.org.uk (search for 'exam stress')

- www.healthforteens.co.uk/feelings/exam-stress

- www.childline.org.uk/info-advice/school-college-and-work/school-college/exam-stress

Read what they say about exam stress and write down:

One new thing you have learned:

One thing you found interesting:

Now imagine you are on an exam support website and you see that someone has posted the message below. What would you write back? Have a go at writing a reply below.

> **Help! I have an exam tomorrow! It's maths and I'm not good at maths! I can't concentrate on my revision, I feel panicky and sick. I've only got a few hours before bed. What shall I do?**

Making Connections

Look back to your worksheet 'Understanding Your Exam Stress'. Notice the arrows in the diagram leading from one shape to the other and back again. This shows us how the shapes connect to each other; our behaviour, thinking, feelings and body sensations all affect each other! Throughout this workbook we explore ideas and strategies that impact on these areas. It is hoped that if we can make a change in one area, it will change other areas too. This idea is based on a cognitive behavioural therapy (CBT) approach.

Let's look again at Oliver's exam stress. The stress is *triggered* by him lying in bed thinking about his SATs practice paper the next day. Shall we try and help him not to *feel* so stressed and worried?

Can you help Oliver *behave* or *act* differently? Write some suggestions for alternative behaviour on the next page in coloured pen.

Can you help Oliver *think* differently? Write some suggestions for alternative thoughts on the next page in coloured pen.

Can you help Oliver experience different *body sensations*? Write some suggestions for alternative body sensations on the next page in coloured pen.

If Oliver is thinking, behaving and experiencing different body sensations, how is he *feeling* now? Write in some new feelings in the box on the next page in coloured pen.

41

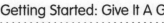

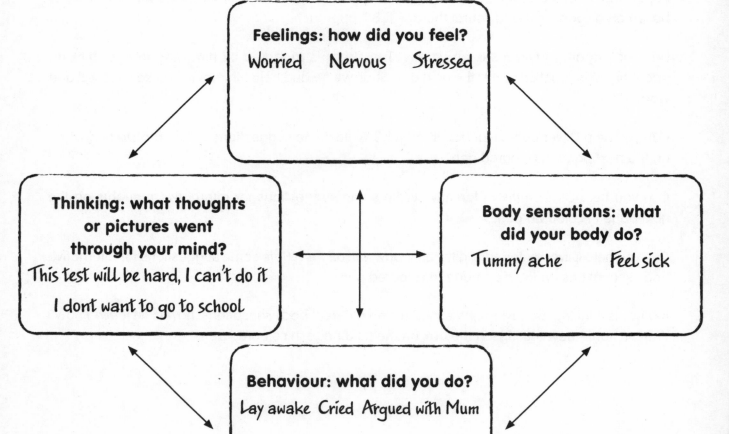

Feelings: how did you feel?
Worried   Nervous   Stressed

Thinking: what thoughts or pictures went through your mind?
This test will be hard, I can't do it
I don't want to go to school

Body sensations: what did your body do?
Tummy ache   Feel sick

Behaviour: what did you do?
Lay awake Cried Argued with Mum

Setting Up Your Study Space

The space or area you study in can be an important factor in managing your exam stress. First you need to work out what kind of environment works best for you and then create that environment (with the help of an adult). Use the multiple-choice questionnaire below to work out your ideal study space. Put a circle around the answer that most applies to you.

1. What level of noise helps you focus?

    Radio on loud   People talking in background   Music on quietly   No noise

2. Where do you prefer to study?

    Bedroom   Lounge   Dining room   Library   Coffee shop

3. What do you like on the wall?

    Blank   Inspiring poster   Revision timetable   Lots of post-it notes

4. What do you like to sit on?

    Sofa   Bed   Office chair   Dining room chair

5. What do you use to lean on?

    My lap   Bed   Table   Desk

6. What do you like to have with you?

    Computer/laptop   Books/notes   Water/snacks   Mobile phone

Now use the Top Tips at the end of this chapter to plan your study space.

Getting Started

Look back through the worksheets you have completed to help answer the questions below.

What are three new things you have learned about exam stress?

1. _____

2. _____

3. _____

What questions do you have about exam stress?

_____

_____

_____

_____

Understanding Exam Stress

Exam stress can affect everyone differently, and many people find themselves feeling worried or under pressure. Lots of young people say they are worried they might fail their exams or not get the results they need for future study or jobs. Here are five top tips to get you started.

1. It is normal to feel stressed or worried about your exams. In fact, experiencing a bit of anxiety (but not too much!) can actually help you perform better during an exam or test.

2. Plan ahead; thinking about your revision and exams in advance should help you to be prepared. You have already made a great start by using this book!

3. Don't ignore the problem by avoiding talking about the exams or revising – this will only make it worse!

4. Make sure you don't forget about the rest of your life during exam time: family, friends, pets, hobbies, sports! It's important to have a balance between study and having fun to help manage stress.

5. Don't forget there is life after exams! This stress won't last forever.

Setting Up Your Study Space

The tips below might help you to design your own study space.

FURNITURE AND EQUIPMENT

- Make sure the chair and table you use are the right height for you, so your feet can be placed flat on the ground and the table is elbow height when sitting down. Try height-adjustable chairs such as office chairs.

- Try using a computer as part of your studying. It doesn't have to all be about reading books or your notes.

- Create space to do some work standing up. This could be standing at the table, working on a high shelf or a whiteboard.

- Have drawers, boxes and shelves to store your things in so that your desk is clear.

- Try and make sure the room is at a comfortable temperature; if the room is too hot or too cold it can be distracting.

VISUAL DISTRACTIONS

- If you are sharing a large table with your brothers, sisters or friends, try screening off a section each.

- Try putting the table or desk against a wall so you are facing a blank space.

- Try using a desk lamp.

- Remove your mobile phone!

SOUND DISTRACTIONS

- Wear headphones with quiet music playing or without any music at all (just to block out the sounds). You could also try disposable ear plugs.

- Find a space away from the TV, radio, road or garden.

- Have set 'quiet times' at home. Can other people wear headphones when watching TV or playing on the computer to help this?

- Remove your mobile phone!

GETTING STARTED: RESOURCES
Books

- *The Teenage Guide to Stress* by Nicola Morgan, 2014, Walker Books.

- *Starving the Anxiety Gremlin: A Cognitive Behavioural Therapy Workbook on Anxiety Management for Young People* by Kate Collins-Donnelly, 2013, Jessica Kingsley Publishers.

- *Starving the Exam Stress Gremlin: A Cognitive Behavioural Therapy Workbook on Managing Exam Stress for Young People* by Kate Collins-Donnelly, 2016, Jessica Kingsley Publishers.

- *The Anxiety Survival Guide for Teens: CBT Skills to Overcome Fear, Worry and Panic* by Jennifer Shannon, 2015, New Harbinger.

Websites

- www.youngminds.org.uk (search for 'exam stress')

- www.healthforteens.co.uk/feelings/exam-stress

- www.childline.org.uk/info-advice/school-college-and-work/school-college/exam-stress

- www.anxietyuk.org.uk

- www.anxietycanada.com/resources/mindshift-app

CHAPTER 3

Looking After Yourself

Looking after yourself is always important, but during the busy times of revision and exams it can easily fall to the bottom of the pile! In this chapter, the focus will be on sleep, exercise and diet and achieving a reasonable work/fun balance.

SLEEP

Every living creature needs to sleep. It is really important as it allows us to develop physically and mentally while our bodies rest. Children aged 5–10 years old need around 10–12 hours' sleep a night and aged 10–12 years need around 10 hours' sleep a night. Young people aged 13–17 years old need around nine hours' sleep a night. Often busy lives mean that this amount of sleep is not achieved. Increasingly, TV, computers, tablets and mobile phones are being used immediately before bedtime. These behaviours are often associated with bedtime resistance, difficulties falling asleep, anxiety around sleep and sleeping fewer hours. We know that if we don't get enough sleep it can affect our concentration, memory, energy, behaviour and mood.

EXERCISE AND DIET

Exercise and a healthy balanced diet are important for the body and mind. Exercise is good for the heart, muscles and bones. Exercise is also good for our mood; during exercise our body makes endorphins, which help us feel good. Research has shown that young people who eat a lot of sugar, fats and processed foods are more likely to experience emotional difficulties. A healthy balanced diet can help young people have good mental health. At times of stress it is common for young people to exercise less and eat less healthy foods and this can lead to even more stress!

BALANCE OF WORK AND FUN

It is important to incorporate time for studying and time for having fun in children and young people's lives. During term time they have already spent around six hours at school learning, so it is essential to have a break from study when they arrive home. It is also important to consider additional organised activities that young people take part in outside school. Many children attend varied sport and music classes, which can positively promote self-confidence and skills. However, too much structured activity can contribute to stress, anxiety and depression in children and young people.

OBJECTIVES

We all experience times when looking after ourselves doesn't take priority, and often these are the times when we need to do it most of all.

The worksheets in this chapter are designed to:

- help the young person reflect on their current sleep, diet, exercise and work/fun balance

- help the young person understand the importance of looking after themselves, particularly during the exam season

- create an opportunity for the young person to identify and try out new ways of looking after themselves.

Are You a Super Sleeper?

Getting enough sleep is a super important part of looking after yourself. Sleep plays a vital role in healthy growth and development. While your body is resting your muscles, bones, skin and brain repair themselves and develop. Sleep also helps you remember what you learn, pay attention and concentrate, solve problems and think of new ideas.

How much sleep do you think a person your age should get every night?

_____

How much sleep do you think you get a night?

_____

If you are not sure how much sleep you get, then complete this sleep diary over the next week to give you a better idea.

Day	Time went to bed	How long it took to fall asleep	Time woke up in morning	Total amount of sleep
Oliver's Example	8.00pm	2hrs	6.35am	7hrs 15mins
Monday				
Tuesday				
Wednesday				
Thursday				
Friday				
Saturday				
Sunday				

If you think your sleep might be a problem, move onto the next worksheet to try and work out why.

Bedtime Habits

Often people have a bedtime routine, which means they usually do the same things in the same order most nights before going to bed and then to sleep. We can get into really good habits that help us fall asleep and sometimes we can end up getting into bad habits that make it harder to fall asleep. Let's find out what your habits are with the quick quiz below.

QUICK QUIZ

Circle your answers to the following questions. Remember to be honest!
Are there any other bedtime habits that you think you have? Add them to the list!

Do you usually go to bed at the same time every night?	Yes	No	Sometimes
Is your bedroom quiet?	Yes	No	Sometimes
Is your bedroom dark?	Yes	No	Sometimes
Do you drink sugary or caffeinated drinks in the evening?	Yes	No	Sometimes
Do you eat a big meal just before bedtime?	Yes	No	Sometimes
Do you have a warm shower or bath before bed?	Yes	No	Sometimes
Do you play on a computer or tablet in the hour before bed?	Yes	No	Sometimes
Do you watch TV in bed?	Yes	No	Sometimes
Do you read a book in bed?	Yes	No	Sometimes
Do you listen to music in bed?	Yes	No	Sometimes
Do you look at your mobile phone in bed?	Yes	No	Sometimes
Do you have a favourite toy or blanket in your bed?	Yes	No	Sometimes
Do you do your homework or study in the hour before bed?	Yes	No	Sometimes
_____	Yes	No	Sometimes
_____	Yes	No	Sometimes
_____	Yes	No	Sometimes

Exercise Check-Up

Getting regular exercise is an essential part of looking after yourself. It plays an important part in helping us feel good and be in a better mood.

How much exercise do you think someone your age should do a week?

_____

How much exercise do you think you do a week?

_____

If you are not sure how much exercise you get a week, fill in the diary below over the next week to help you work it out.

Day	Before school/ morning	During school/ daytime	After school/ afternoon	Evening	Total amount of exercise
Aiden's Example	Playground 10mins	PE lesson 1hr	Swimming lesson 30mins	Walk dog 15mins	1hr 55mins
Monday					
Tuesday					
Wednesday					
Thursday					
Friday					
Saturday					
Sunday					

Exercise Experiment

Write in the bubble below how you are feeling at the moment, as you sit filling in these worksheets. Think about how much energy you have, how your body is feeling and what kind of mood you are in.

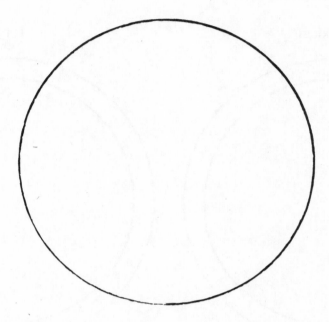

Do five minutes of exercise NOW! You could run on the spot, do star jumps, go on the trampoline (if there is one nearby) or do push-ups.

Now write in the bubble how you are feeling. Again, think about how much energy you have, how your body is feeling and what kind of mood you are in.

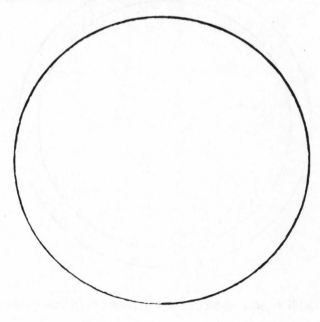

Dishes of the Day

Eating a healthy balanced diet can help you feel good in your mood and help you concentrate better. Let's think about your eating habits by drawing or writing on the plates below your favourite breakfast, lunch and dinner.

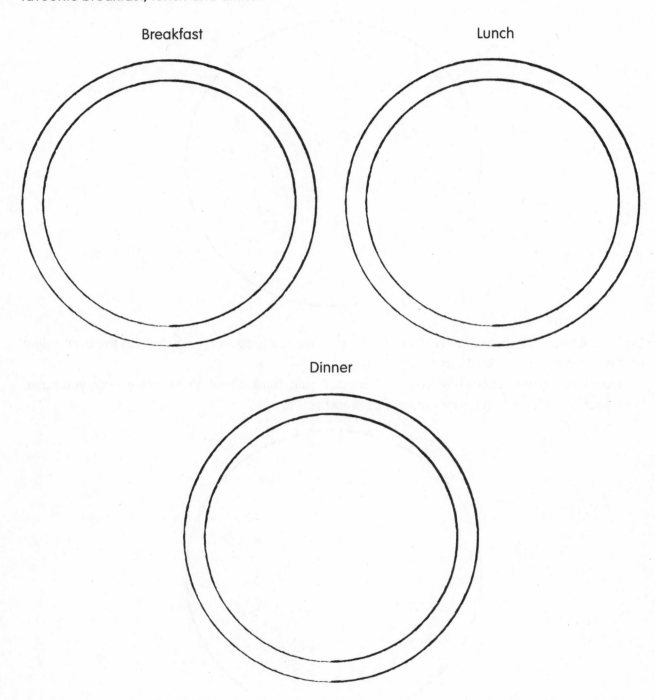

Do you think these are healthy meal choices? If not, how could you make them a little healthier?

Balancing Act

Do you think you have a good balance of work and fun in your life?

- Evenings (circle answer)   YES   NO

- Weekends (circle answer)   YES   NO

- School holidays (circle answer)   YES   NO

What is the impact of this? Write in the explosion shape below the things that annoy you about spending so much time studying or very little time studying. For example, you don't get to spend time with people you care about, or you get into trouble at school for not doing school work.

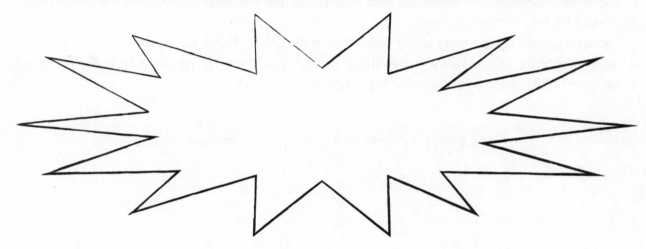

Speak to two people (parents, friends, family, teachers, sports coach) and find out what they think the downside is of not balancing work and fun. Write down their answers in the explosion shapes below.

Sleep: The Golden Hour

Read through 'Top Tips for Young People' on Sleep at the end of this chapter and find out about the golden hour.

Review your Bedtime Habits quiz – do you think that you already have a relaxing, calm, technology-free golden hour before bed most nights? If yes, then you can skip this worksheet!

If you think you could improve on your golden hour, then read on! It can be hard to get rid of bad habits and start with new ones. Often what helps us get through these changes is thinking about a reward or good thing that could be enjoyed at the end. These thoughts go like this…so maybe if I leave my technology downstairs every day this week I'll be able to watch a film at the weekend. If I go to bed 20 minutes earlier, I will feel less tired tomorrow. If I use my new bedtime routine, my parents will be really happy with me and I might get a treat!

So what improvements do you need to make at bedtime to help you achieve the golden hour (routine, relaxed, technology free)?

What reward or good thing could come from you making these changes?

Use the table below to interview three people you know to discover how they reward themselves after doing a boring or horrible activity.

Name	Boring/Horrible task	Reward

Exercise Planner

I expect you know by now that exercise can really help you feel happier, concentrate well when you are studying and keep you healthy. Think about the sorts of exercise or activities that you like to do. It could be anything from swimming, jumping on the trampoline, doing push-ups, playing football to playing interactive movement-based computer games. Fill out the exercise plan below to help you think about the best times for you to exercise and if you can find someone to exercise with.

_____'s Exercise Plan			
Time of day	**Activities**	**Time needed**	**Person to join me**
Before school			
Lunch time			
After school			
Evening			
Weekend			

Getting an Equal Balance

You will know from the 'Balancing Act' worksheet whether you have a good balance of study and fun in your life. Using the balancing scales below and on the next page, plan how you will get a good balance of fun and study. Lily has completed one to give you some ideas.

Lily's Weekend Scale

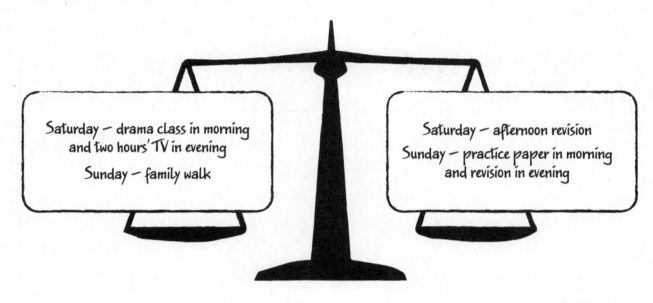

Saturday – drama class in morning and two hours' TV in evening

Sunday – family walk

Saturday – afternoon revision

Sunday – practice paper in morning and revision in evening

After school/evenings

Getting an Equal Balance Continued

Weekends

Holidays

What Could I Do If…?

Imagine yourself in the situations below, and think about how you might respond using the ideas you have learned from this chapter of the book.

Situation 1

Every evening you seem to get into a massive argument with your parents over going to bed. They keep nagging you, telling you to go to bed earlier and to stop playing on your console. This makes you really stressed out as you have spent all day at school and you feel as if you deserve some relaxation time. You also worry that if you switch off the console earlier you will miss out on things with your friends who talk online as they play; they might also call you a baby for going offline early. What could you do?

_____

_____

_____

Situation 2

It's only four weeks to go until your exams and you are revising as much as you can in the evenings and at the weekends. You have stopped doing all your hobbies and meeting up with friends as you want to focus on your exams. You are feeling very stressed out; all you can think about are your exams and what will happen if you don't get the results your teachers have predicted. Your friend asks you out for an ice cream for their birthday, and you can see they are upset when you say no. How could you try to improve the situation?

_____

_____

_____

Looking After Yourself

Look back through the worksheets you have completed to help you answer the questions below.

Do you get enough sleep and have good bedtime habits? (circle answer)   YES   NO

Do you have a healthy balanced diet? (circle answer)   YES   NO

Do you exercise regularly? (circle answer)   YES   NO

Do you have a good balance of work and fun? (circle answer)   YES   NO

My top three strategies to help me look after myself are:

1. _____

2. _____

3. _____

Would looking after myself be a good area to work on?

Young person:	Yes ☐	No ☐	Maybe ☐
Adult:	Yes ☐	No ☐	Maybe ☐

If YES or MAYBE, see Chapter 10 for help with goal setting.

Sleep

It is fairly common to have problems with sleeping occasionally and particularly at times of stress such as exam time. It is important to know how much sleep you should try to get each night.

Age	Sleep per night
5–10 years	10–12 hours
10–12 years	10 hours
13–17 years	9 hours
Adults	7–9 hours

You may be wondering why sleep is connected to exam stress. Sleep is important for many reasons including the following:

- If you don't get enough sleep it can be harder to concentrate; this is the last thing you need during tests or exams!

- You are more likely to feel sad or down in your mood when you are tired.

- Getting a good night's sleep can help you cope better with stressful situations such as tests or exams.

GOOD HABITS

Please consider trying out these good bedtime habits – it really will be worth it!

Routine

A good routine can really help you fall asleep. Try to have the same bedtime and wake-up time every day; this means no very long lie in at the weekend. Also try to follow the same relaxing routine each night before bed; perhaps have a bath, read a book (not a school book!) and listen to some relaxing music. You could even try a relaxation or mindfulness exercise from later in this book.

Bedroom atmosphere

Do you find your bedroom comfortable and relaxing? It's important that your mattress and bedding are comfy, that your room is the right temperature and is dark enough. It is also important that you have a quiet and calm bedroom space. If any of these things are a problem, try and let your parents know.

Technology

Research has shown that using screens in the hour before bed can double the time it takes you to fall asleep. The bright lights of the screens on laptops, computers, tablets, mobile phones and televisions can stop your brain from releasing a hormone called melatonin. Melatonin's job is to make you sleepy before bed. Don't use your technology in the hour before bed; this is called the golden hour as it's so important. If this is very difficult, start with not using it for 10 minutes before bed, then 20 minutes, until you have reached the golden hour. Some young people leave their technology downstairs or in a different room to stop them being tempted to use it in the night.

Night Night!

Looking After Yourself Too!

It is very likely that you have been telling your young person all the advice in this chapter for a long time! Eat healthily! Do exercise! Stop playing on your phone/console! Go out and have some fun with your friends! It's not easy to implement though, particularly in the teenage years. I hope the worksheets in this book promote a journey of self-discovery and collaboration which will facilitate some change or at least contemplation of change. It is important to try and get a balance between setting boundaries and limits, giving encouragement and rewards and allowing young people to learn from their mistakes. That's quite a balancing act!

It's also important to set a good example. Consider your own sleep, eating and exercise habits and your work/relaxation balance. Perhaps if you feel you also need to make changes in your life you could join your young person with some shared targets. Often it can help with motivation if you have a partner you are working with, so it could be a win-win scenario for you both!

LOOKING AFTER YOURSELF: RESOURCES
Books

- *The Sleep Book: How to Sleep Well Every Night* by Guy Meadows, 2014, Orion.

- *Eating Mindfully for Teens: A Workbook to Help You Make Healthy Choices, End Emotional Eating, and Feel Great* by Susan Albers, 2018, New Harbinger.

- *The Food Parade: Healthy Eating with the Nutritious Food Groups* by Elicia Castaldi, 2013, Henry Holt & Company.

- *Blame My Brain*, Chapter 2 'Sleep' by Nicola Morgan, 2013, Walker Books.

Websites

- www.teen-sleep.org.uk

- https://youngminds.org.uk/find-help/feelings-and-symptoms/sleep-problems

CHAPTER 4

Doing Things Differently

As you have just discovered in Chapter 2, behaviour can impact on feelings, thoughts and body sensations. The focus of this chapter is on behaviour – how exam stress can impact on our behaviour and also how behaviour can impact on exam stress.

Typically, stress is demonstrated through behaviour; young people may be more prone to crying, act like a younger child, sleep more or less than usual, withdraw from those around them or argue more with people. They might even develop fixed rituals or routines, start to miss school, self-harm, drink alcohol or take drugs. These behaviours can often lead to further stress, creating a vicious circle.

During difficult times, such as exam season, symptoms of stress can rise significantly. It is important to promote positive ways to monitor, detect and manage these difficult feelings at an early stage. Young people can often seem to overreact to situations and emotions and can switch to 'fight or flight' responses. They find it difficult to calm themselves down. These difficult feelings can lead to aggressive or avoidant behaviour if not managed effectively.

We all develop different strategies to manage stress in our lives, and children and young people are at the start of this journey and still finding out what works for them. It is good to try out different strategies as we all have our preferences.

OBJECTIVES

Whether we are aware of it or not, we have all learned and adopted strategies to help us manage our stress. Some strategies are more effective than others and some are hard to recognise until we sit down and think about them. The worksheets and tip sheets in this chapter are designed to:

- help the young person understand that everyone experiences stress and that we all need to learn to manage stress

- help the young person learn about how their behaviour changes when they are experiencing exam stress

- enable you and the young person to identify and try out strategies that help them remain calm during revision and exams and to start practising them.

Stress Volcano

Exam stress can be like a volcano – when you feel calm there is no smoke or lava, and then when you start to 'rumble' (get annoyed or wound up), smoke starts to appear and the lava bubbles inside. When you 'explode', the volcano erupts with smoke, lava and rocks that go everywhere! Next to the three pictures below and on the next page, write about what happens to your behaviour when you get stressed. Aiden has started this worksheet to help you out, so highlight his points if you think they also apply to you, and underneath add your own.

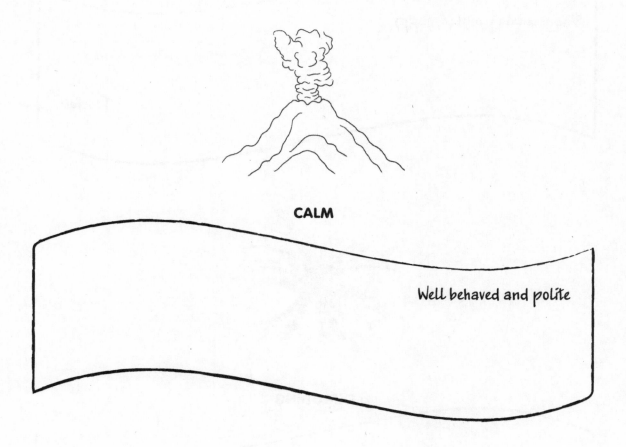

CALM

Well behaved and polite

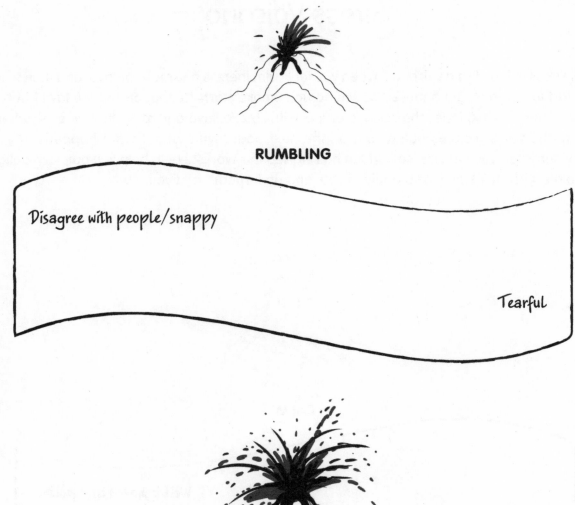

RUMBLING

Disagree with people/snappy

Tearful

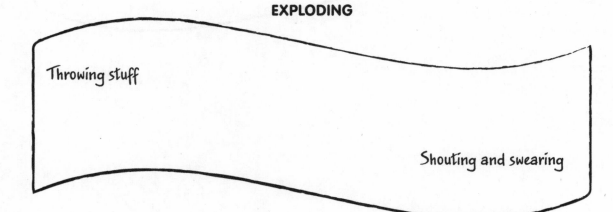

EXPLODING

Throwing stuff

Shouting and swearing

When I Get Stressed I...

You have started to think about what you might do at different stages of feeling 'stressed'. Some of these things may be in the table below – place a tick next to each one that you do, and a cross next to the ones that you don't. Are there any other ways that you cope with exam stress? Add them to the list too.

   Once you have finished filling in the sheet about yourself, try to 'interview' two other people (friends or family) and see how they respond when they get stressed.

When I get stressed I...	Me:	Name:	Name:
Shout			
Walk away			
Say things I regret			
Talk over the top of people			
Hit or push			
Ignore people			
Bite my nails			
Give up trying			
Listen to music			
Hang out in my room			
Cry			

What Helps to Calm Me Down?

Whether we realise it or not, we all use strategies to help us calm down in times of stress. Look through the examples Lily, Aiden and Oliver have put together. If you have used any of these ideas and they have helped, highlight the words in coloured pen. Add any extra ideas about what has helped you to chill out in the 'thought bubble'.

Reading   Going somewhere quiet

Laughing   Playing a game on your console

Talking it through   Playing with a pet

Listening to music   Having a bath or shower

Singing or whistling   Exercise or playing sports

Going for a walk   Taking deep breaths

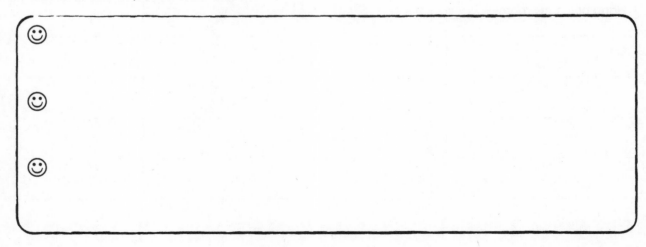

Do some research on the internet about popular ways to calm down when people feel stressed. Write down what you find out below.

☺

☺

☺

Stress Busters

Try each of these exercises and rate whether they could help you manage stress while it is still at the 'rumbling' stage. Are they good (thumbs up), okay (thumb sideways) or not for you (thumbs down)? It is good to a have a range of stress busters so you can chose one that suits you in different places (at home, at school, in the car, at the sports club) and depending on what mood you are in. It may take a while to get the equipment together, so you might want to spread this exercise out across a few sessions.

Make those muscles work!

Slurp and suck: Have a drink from a sports bottle or drink from a cup using a straw.	👍	👉	👎
Push-ups: Try these on the floor, against the wall, on the chair (push down on the seat and lift up bottom). Keep going until you can't do any more!	👍	👉	👎
Blowing: Take a deep breath and then put something to your lips so you have to blow hard to get air around it, maybe a pen or your fingers. Repeat 5–10 times.	👍	👉	👎
Push, pull or squeeze: Push using a hand or foot pump, 'rowing' exercises using an elastic yoga band, squeeze a large ball of Blu-Tack/Plasticine/Theraputty.	👍	👉	👎
Chew, crunch or suck on food: Try raisins, carrots, celery, pretzels, gum. Suck on hard sweets (try sugarless ones!)	👍	👉	👎

Touchy feely!

Fidget with different objects. Try: • squeezing (e.g. Blu-Tack, stress ball) • wrapping (e.g. pipe cleaner/lace around fingers) • stretching (e.g. hairband, elastic band, charity bracelet) • feeling (e.g. textured ball, slime, key ring).	👍	👉	👎
Vibration: Use a vibrating massager or cushion on your arms/body. (Warning: some people don't like this feeling so maybe try an electric toothbrush as a test.)	👍	👉	👎
Get comfy: Try different positions that give your body lots of calming touch: lie on your back or tummy on the floor, sit in a beanbag/armchair, and have cushions to use as well. Try combining this with other strategies.	👍	👉	👎
Hand massage: Use your thumb to massage the palm of your other hand. Press firmly. Gradually work up each finger in long strokes, then change hands.	👍	👉	👎

Have a laugh!

Movie scene: Find one of your favourite funny scenes in a movie and memorise it so that you can 'play' it in your head and make yourself laugh.	👍	✋	👎
Joke of the day: Write down a few jokes that make you laugh or find some funny pictures.	👍	✋	👎

Sound and light show!

Separate space: Find a space without too many things to look at – the corner of a room, lying down looking at the ceiling. Try combining this with music and/or a fidget.	👍	✋	👎
Music: Listen to music that you find relaxing and that has a steady beat and melody. You may want to try some specific relaxation music. Consider using earphones to block out the background noise. Some people like just earphones without the music!	👍	✋	👎
Images: Look at something calming such as fish in an aquarium, lava lamp, glitter wand, fibre optic light, YouTube video of waves or patterns.	👍	✋	👎

Have a Break

If you are finding you are feeling stressed about your school work, particularly when you are doing homework or revision, perhaps you need to have a break! It's important to schedule in regular breaks and make these breaks fun and rewarding. The break doesn't have to take long – ten minutes can work really well.

Lily has started a list of ten-minute break activities; add your own ideas and then next time you are doing revision or homework make sure that for every 30–45 minutes of study you have a ten-minute break. Further information on movement breaks during exams can be found in Chapter 8.

Lily's Ten-Minute Breaks

- Put on some music
- Go for a short walk
- Practise a brief mindfulness exercise (Chapter 6)
- Have a soft drink
- Have a healthy snack
- Chat to a friend/family member
- Read a magazine
-
-
-
-

Creating a Chill-Out Space

Chill-out spaces are calm, safe and comfortable areas that help you relax and refocus. They are somewhere to go when you feel the first signs of stress (rumbling) in order to stop the stress or volcano erupting. Revision or school work should *never* be done in your chill-out space! Chill-out spaces can be made anywhere, including school. This activity focuses on creating one at home.

This is what you need to do:

1. Create a plan of what you think you need to do – use the table on the next page to help you do this.

2. Show your parents/carers your plan. Check if your plan could work, or together come up with some alternatives. Go through the 'Tips' below and agree some guidelines on how you will use the space.

3. Try it for a week or two at home and then fill in the 'report card' at the end.

TIPS

*   Avoid putting games or technology into the space – it isn't a second bedroom!

*   You should never be forced to use the chill-out area. It is not a time-out or punishment space.

*   You can choose to go there whenever you want, but you may need to set a rough time limit on how long to spend in there.

*   Agree the ways in which your parents or carers can suggest that it might be helpful to use the space (e.g. 'how about five minutes to chill out' or use a signal you have agreed together).

*   Add any extra family rules you might need.

Plan for creating a chill-out space

Step	What I need to do	Plan	Tick when done
Where	Chose a space away from busy areas (e.g. the corner of room, spare room).		
Privacy	Screen your space as much as possible (e.g. a mini-tent, use furniture).		
Comfy	Add beanbags, cushions, chairs, blankets.		
Stress busters	Add up to three things from 'Stress Busters' activity.		
Relaxation/ mindfulness	Use some of the ideas from the next chapter; print out a relaxation sheet or use music.		
Who	Decide if this space is just for you or if anyone in the family can use it.		

REPORT CARD FOR CHILL-OUT SPACE

From The International Institute of Chill-Out Spaces

REPORT CARD FOR _____ **FAMILY**

Date: _____

1. Did the chill-out space get set up?   Yes / No

2. How many times was the chill-out space used?   _____ in the week

3. Overall rating for the family having 'Given It A Go'   A / B / C / D

4. Did you like spending time in the chill-out space?   Yes / No / Sometimes

5. Did you find it relaxing?   Yes / No / Sometimes

6. Overall rating for the space and how well it worked   A / B / C / D

Comments and suggestions:

_____

_____

_____

Signed: _____

Talking Things Through

If you are feeling worried or anxious, it can be helpful to talk things through with a friend, someone in your family or another adult like a teacher, youth worker or school nurse. Sometimes talking to someone else can help you feel better or they might come up with different ideas you haven't thought of. Have a think using this worksheet about who you could try and talk to when you are feeling stressed. Some people really aren't good at talking, so see if you can think of any alternative ways to share feelings – maybe keeping a diary or using an online forum.

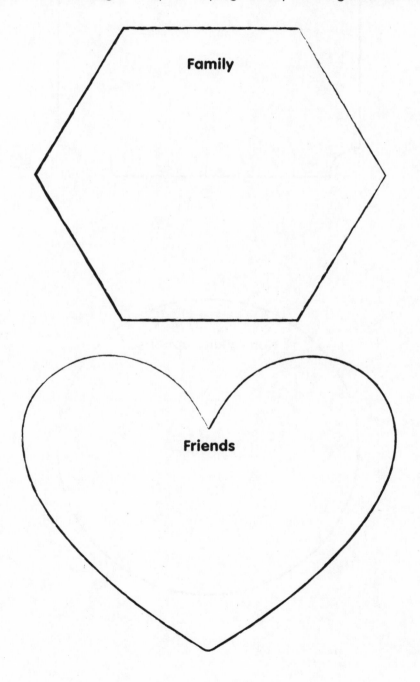

Other adults

Non-talking options

Doing Things Differently!

Think about a situation that happened recently, one that ended up with you getting stressed – perhaps you had a test, were revising or talking to your friends or family about exams. Fill out the boxes below, thinking about what *did* happen and then what *could* have happened if you had done things differently (maybe using some ideas from this chapter).

 What DID happen?

 What COULD have happened?

What did you DO to deal with it? (What did you do/say?)	**What could you DO next time to deal with it?** (What could you have done/said? What stress busters could you have used?)

What was the outcome? (How did it end up? Good and bad points?)	**What could the outcome have been?** (How could it have ended up? Good and bad points)

What Could I Do If...?

Imagine yourself in the situations below and think about how you might respond using the ideas you have learned from this chapter of the book.

Situation 1

It is the weekend, you have five exams next week, you have been revising all morning and are feeling really stressed about how much you have still got to do. Your brother wants you to come out with him and walk the dog, but you shout at him to go away as you have too much to do. What can you do to calm yourself down so that you can still get some revision done?

_____

_____

_____

Situation 2

You are lying in bed finding it hard to fall asleep. You are feeling worried about getting your science test results at school tomorrow. You are a bit tearful and wish you could miss school tomorrow. You think that you have done badly in the test, as it was pretty hard. What can you do to calm yourself down so that you can fall asleep?

_____

_____

_____

Doing Things Differently

Look back through the worksheets you have completed to help answer the questions below.

How do I know when I am starting to get stressed?

_____

_____

_____

What are my top three strategies to chill out?

1. _____

2. _____

3. _____

Would doing things differently be a good area to work on?

Young person:	Yes ☐	No ☐	Maybe ☐
Adult:	Yes ☐	No ☐	Maybe ☐

If YES or MAYBE, see Chapter 10 for help with goal setting.

Managing Stress

I have outlined some top tips on simple ways that you can help support young people to manage their stress in everyday situations.

- *Timing.* It is vital to remember that strategies should only be used at the early 'rumbling' stages of stress. Once the young person is 'exploding', no strategy will be effective, and time and space are typically the only appropriate responses. Using strategies at this time can be problematic – adults give up on good strategies as they seem ineffective and young people come to dislike the techniques because they associate them with being upset.

- *Lead by example.* Spend some time thinking about your own responses to stress. Often we could all do with improving our skills in handling stress – it could be a good idea to practise some of the strategies in this book alongside the young person! The more you are in control of your own stress, the more able you are to support others. It is also helpful for young people to realise that learning and refining these skills is something we all need to do.

- *Stay calm.* Any signs of anxiety or frustration shown by you will only increase the young person's stress levels. Check your voice and body language.

- *Learn the warning signs.* Identify the early signs of stress that are unique to the young person (the 'rumbling' stage). Intervening at this point in order to prevent the build-up of stress is much easier than dealing with the 'explosion'.

- *Don't add demands.* When you detect early signs of stress, make sure you do not add extra demands on the young person or remind them of all the things they should be doing. Instead, use some of the strategies from this book as a form of short break or give them space or reduce their demands. The priority is to avoid escalation.

- *Use humour.* This can help to quickly change the mood and gives the young person some breathing space in which they may be able to regain control.

DOING THINGS DIFFERENTLY: RESOURCES
Books

- *Starving the Anger Gremlin: A Cognitive Behavioural Workbook on Anger Management for Young People* by Kate Collins-Donnelly, 2012, Jessica Kingsley Publishers.

- *A Volcano in My Tummy: Helping Children to Handle Anger* by E. Whitehouse and W. Pudney, 1998, New Society Publishers.

Websites

- www.alertprogram.com
- www.relaxkids.com

CHAPTER 5

Thinking About Thinking

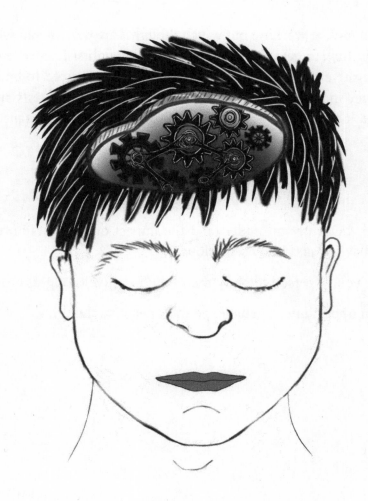

Thinking About Thinking: Introducing

In Chapter 2 we briefly explored the cognitive behavioural model. In this chapter, we are going to focus on the 'cognitive' or thinking part. Our thoughts can have a significant effect on our feelings, behaviour and body sensations. How we interpret and make sense of situations and experiences can have a big impact, so it is important to stop and think about our thinking. If we manage to work on our unhelpful thoughts, it can change the way we feel and behave.

The first part of thinking about thinking is helping the young person identify what a thought is and how it affects their feelings, behaviour and body sensations. This is not always as easy as it sounds, particularly for younger children (around 7 years and under) or if a young person has autism spectrum condition or a learning disability. So, take time to go over how to identify a thought and how a thought is different from a behaviour or an emotion.

We will then look at working out which thoughts are helpful and which are unhelpful and, importantly, how to get rid of those unhelpful thoughts! These exercises are not about replacing all negative thoughts with positive ones – we do need to be realistic, we aren't living in a Disney movie! We need to acknowledge that exams, tests and revision can be challenging and it's how we cope with that challenge that's important.

OBJECTIVES

The worksheets and advice sheets in this chapter are designed to:

- help the young person understand the impact of thoughts on the way they feel, their behaviour and body sensations

- help the young person identify their own negative thoughts around exam stress

- create an opportunity to challenge their negative thoughts.

Worry Thoughts

The way we think is super important as it affects how we feel and behave.

Have a look at the thoughts below. Do any of these apply to you when you think about your exam stress? Colour in those that apply to you and add any extras in the empty boxes.

I'm going to fail	I should have done more revision	If I mess these exams up, I won't get to university and will never get a job
All my friends are bound to do well	My dad will be so upset with me and think I'm useless	I really can't do this
If I don't do well in my exams, I may as well be dead	I hate revising, it's so boring, I can't be bothered	I am the most stupid person I know
What if I don't get the grades I need? It will be terrible	I expect everyone else did better than me in this test	
If I don't do well in this test, everyone will think I'm stupid		I feel so tired and sick I can't do this today
My mum always said I wouldn't do well – she was right	I won't know the answer to one question	My life is over
	I always do badly in tests, so why even try?	No one else is studying, so I don't need to either

Think/Feel/Behave Quiz

Can you work out whether the statements below are thoughts, feelings or behaviour? Tick which box you think each statement should go into. See how many you can get right (answers are at the end of the chapter).

Statement	Thoughts	Feelings	Behaviour
Stay in bed			
Stressed			
I am going to fail			
Confused			
Crying			
Put off doing something			
I'm rubbish			
Angry			
Avoid meeting up with friends			
Embarrassed			
Skip school/college			
I'm useless and a waste of space			
Make mistakes			
People think I am stupid			
Guilty			
Lonely			
If I don't pass these exams, I will never get a job			
I hate being me			
Overwhelmed			
Miss eating breakfast			
My friends think I am an idiot			

Thinking Traps

Now you are aware of your thoughts when you are feeling stressed or anxious, the next step is to look closely at them and check whether they are helpful or not. Often, we all fall into thinking traps, where our thoughts become quite unhelpful and can make us feel even more stressed or anxious. Have a look at these thinking traps and decide whether this has ever happened to you and how often. Use your answers from the 'Worry Thoughts' worksheet to help you.

Thinking error	Description and example	Often	Sometimes	Not really
Blaming yourself	Thinking that everything that goes wrong is your fault. **'It's my fault the whole class got detention'**			
Ignoring the good	Paying lots of attention to the bad things and ignoring when something good happens. **'Even though I had a good morning, it's the worst day ever as Emma and I fell out'**			
Fortune telling	Thinking that you will know what will happen in the future and that it will be bad. **'I am going to fail my exams no matter what I do'**			
Blowing things up	Making a really big deal out of something small that has happened. **'I got two maths questions wrong. I am the worst at maths and am going to fail this year'**			
Mind reading	Believing you know what someone else is thinking or why they are doing something, when you don't have this information. **'My French teacher thinks I am stupid and I will do really badly in this test'**			
Should statements	Believing that things have to be a certain way. **'I should always be totally calm'**			

Thinking error	Description and example	Often	Sometimes	Not really
Putting yourself down	Having a negative belief about yourself and applying it to everything. **'I'm so stupid, everything I say and do is wrong'**			
Miss/Mr Perfect	Thinking you must be perfect in everything you do, otherwise you are useless. **'If I don't get an A in every exam, I am an idiot'**			
What if thinking	Thinking that bad things will happen and jumping ahead to what that will mean. **'What if I fail my exams? My life will be over'**			

Thoughts Are Not Facts

It is important to be aware that your thoughts are just thoughts and nothing more. They are not facts, but we often treat them as if they are! So once you have learned to notice your thoughts and had a think about the thinking traps you are falling into, you can start to challenge them. Try to challenge your thoughts by asking yourself these questions.

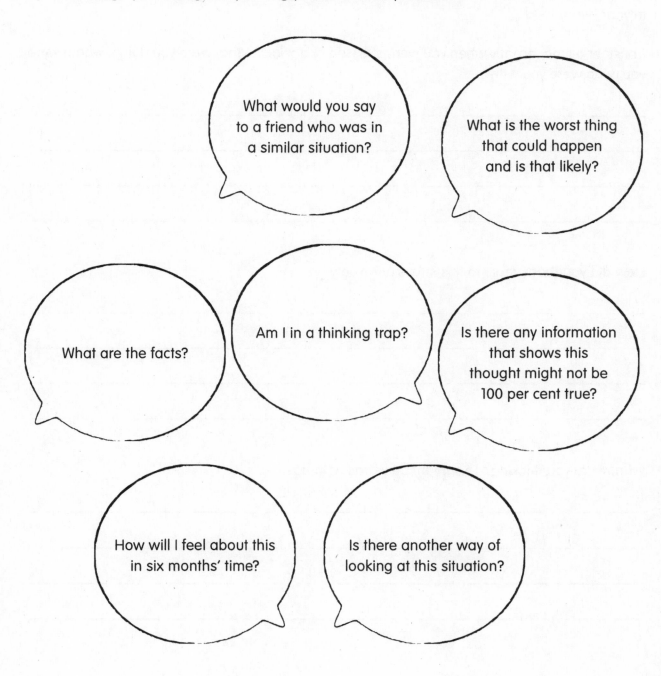

Thought Challenging Practice

Challenging thoughts is quite a skill and takes practice, just like riding a bike, driving a car or learning a new sport. This worksheet will guide you through the process of challenging your thoughts, using everything you have learned so far in this chapter. Once you have done this a few times, you might not need the worksheet as you might be able to remember how to do this in your head.

Consider a time recently when you were stressed or anxious. What were you doing, where were you, who were you with?

_____

_____

_____

_____

How did your body react to this stress or anxiety?

_____

_____

_____

_____

What were you thinking? This might be words or images.

_____

_____

_____

_____

Use the questions from 'Thoughts Are Not Facts' to challenge your thoughts. Show how you have done this in the box below.

How can you think differently?

_____

_____

_____

_____

Ruminations

Ruminations are unhelpful thoughts that go round and round and round in your head. They can make you feel very stressed and anxious. You may not experience this, in which case skip this worksheet! If you do find you have the same old thoughts coming back a lot of the time, then you might want to read on for some ways to help.

- Distract yourself from your thoughts; do some exercise or a fun activity with friends or family.

- Stop those thoughts! When you notice that the same thought is on your mind, tell yourself STOP or NO!

- Write it down or draw it; sometimes getting your thoughts down on paper can help relieve them.

- Share your thoughts with someone you trust; choose someone who will help you talk them through and not make you worry more!

- Plan some worry time, allow yourself a fixed period of time to worry (15 minutes after school), and the chances are the time will come and you won't feel like worrying.

- Meditate; see the next chapter for details on mindfulness exercises and meditation.

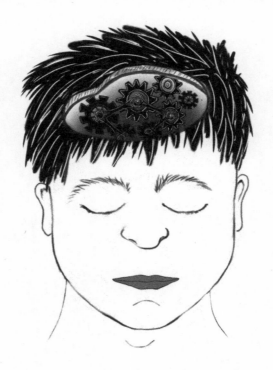

Positive Self-Talk

It is important to learn how to encourage yourself when faced with a difficult task. Sometimes, things like doing some revision or taking a test or exam can be very daunting.

One way of dealing with this is to say positive, helpful things to yourself. Professional sportsmen and women do this all the time so that they play their best and don't give up when things get difficult. You could make a flashcard with a couple of phrases on it that work for you. You could keep this in your diary, pencil case or pocket. Here are some phrases that other people have found useful. Try and add two of your own in the empty thought bubbles below.

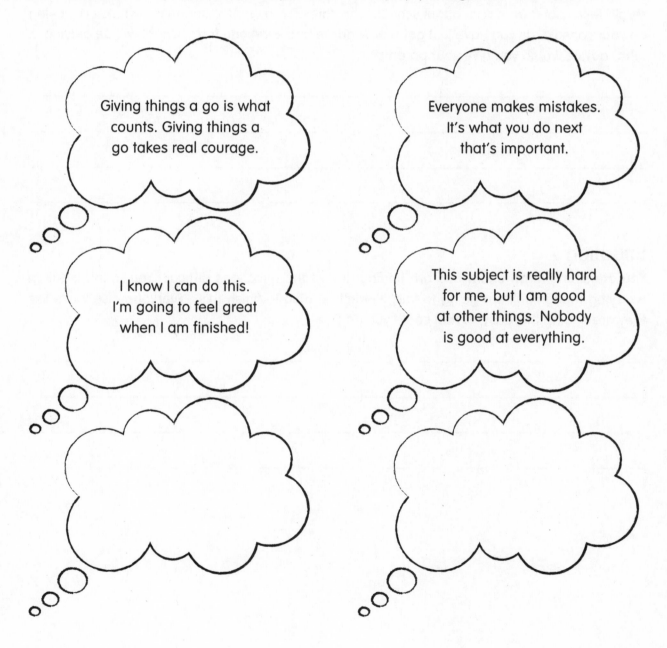

Giving things a go is what counts. Giving things a go takes real courage.

Everyone makes mistakes. It's what you do next that's important.

I know I can do this. I'm going to feel great when I am finished!

This subject is really hard for me, but I am good at other things. Nobody is good at everything.

What Could I Do If...?

Imagine yourself in the situations below. Think about how you might respond using the ideas you have learned from this chapter of the book.

Situation 1

You have a test at school next week and your parents think you should spend some time at the weekend revising. You don't really feel like it and find yourself thinking, 'I don't care about this stupid test, I don't even care about school, who cares?' You want to spend the weekend playing on your console, as you have just got a new game and everyone from school will be playing it. What advice would you give your parents?

_____

_____

_____

_____

Situation 2

You are sitting in an exam and are finding one of the questions difficult. Your mind is full of worrying thoughts: 'I am going to fail', 'I won't be able to finish this', 'Everyone else looks like they are finding this easy.' What could you do?

_____

_____

_____

_____

Thinking About Thinking

Look back through the worksheets you have completed to help answer the questions below.

What are some of the unhelpful thoughts you have about exams or tests?

_____

_____

_____

Do you sometime fall into thinking traps? If so, which ones?

_____

_____

_____

Name one strategy to help you manage your thinking.

_____

_____

_____

Would doing thinking about thinking be a good area to work on?

Young person:	Yes ☐	No ☐	Maybe ☐
Adult:	Yes ☐	No ☐	Maybe ☐

If YES or MAYBE, see Chapter 10 for help with goal setting.

Supporting Thinking About Thinking

Children and young people who experience significant anxiety will be more likely to think about things in a particular way. They are more likely to:

- be 'on the lookout' for danger or threat

- jump to conclusions about what is happening

- interpret situations as threatening

- think they can't cope with dangers.

It is important to try and understand what the anxious child or young person is thinking. Try asking them directly while the worries are happening or later on when they are calmer. Make sure you keep an open mind about what they might be worried about rather than assuming you know. If they are finding it difficult to talk about their worries, you might need to make some suggestions yourself.

'Why are you worried?'
'What do you think will happen?'
'What is making you nervous?'

Once thoughts are identified, you can begin to support the young person to challenge their thinking. Help them consider whether their thought is helpful or not and whether it is realistic or not.

'Has that happened before?'
'How likely is it that it will happen?'
'What makes you think that it will happen?'

The next step is to support the young person to consider alternative ways to think about the situation. Try to encourage them to take a different point of view. Do this through asking questions rather than telling them what to think.

'Is there another way of looking at this?'
'What would a friend say to you?'
'What would you say to a friend in the same situation?'

THINKING ABOUT THINKING: RESOURCES
Books

- *Starving the Anxiety Gremlin: A Cognitive Behavioural Therapy Workbook on Anxiety Management for Young People* by Kate Collins-Donnelly, 2013, Jessica Kingsley Publishers.

- *Think Good – Feel Good: A Cognitive Behaviour Therapy Workbook for Children and Young People* by Paul Stallard, 2002, Wiley Blackwell.

- *Conquer Negative Thinking for Teens: A Workbook to Break the Nine Thought Habits That Are Holding You Back* by Mary Karapetian Alvord and Anne McGrath, 2017, New Harbinger.

Websites

- www.stressbusting.co.uk/cognitive-bias-modification

- www.brave-online.com

- www.moodgym.com.au

THINK/FEEL/BEHAVE QUIZ ANSWERS

Statement	Thoughts	Feelings	Behaviour
Stay in bed			✓
Stressed		✓	
I am going to fail	✓		
Confused		✓	
Crying			✓
Put off doing something			✓
I'm rubbish	✓		
Angry		✓	
Avoid meeting up with friends			✓
Embarrassed		✓	
Skip school/college			✓
I'm useless and a waste of space	✓		
Make mistakes			✓
People think I am stupid	✓		
Guilty		✓	
Lonely		✓	
If I don't pass these exams, I will never get a job	✓		
I hate being me	✓		
Overwhelmed		✓	
Miss eating breakfast			✓
My friends think I am an idiot	✓		

CHAPTER 6

Mindfulness

Mindfulness is becoming increasingly popular as a technique to manage stress and anxiety for children and young people, as well as adults. Some schools incorporate mindfulness exercises during the school day or offer clubs at lunchtime or after school.

Mindfulness is awareness of the present moment. It means living in the present moment without judging or ignoring anything or getting caught up in the stresses of life. Mindfulness brings calmness and also awareness.

Mindfulness can bring about feelings of calmness in the body and mind. As you are aware from Chapter 2, body, thoughts, emotions and behaviour all interconnect, so by making these positive changes to body and mind there is likely to be an impact on emotions and behaviour too.

Exam stress can often be felt in the body as well as in behaviour and thinking. Stress or anxiety can affect the body in many ways such as stomach aches, headaches, trouble breathing, upset stomach, problems with sleep, feeling dizzy, changes to appetite, unable to sit still, chest pains or general aches and pains.

There is considerable research and evidence to show that practising mindfulness exercises regularly can reduce stress and anxiety, improve the memory and increase focus and concentration. Mindfulness is fast becoming a life skill as well as an important strategy to manage stress such as exams.

OBJECTIVES

The worksheets and tip sheets in this chapter are designed to:

- help the young person understand the concept of mindfulness

- help the young person try out mindfulness exercises that are effective in reducing stress and start practising these in everyday life

- enable the young person to reflect and try out other activities that promote a mindful approach.

Body Stress

Our bodies can show signs that we are stressed out. Lily has started to label the drawing below to display how her body shows she is stressed. Can you add your labels in a different colour to this drawing? If you are working in a group, it can be fun to get a giant outline drawing of a body on a large piece of paper and then all label your stress symptoms in different colours.

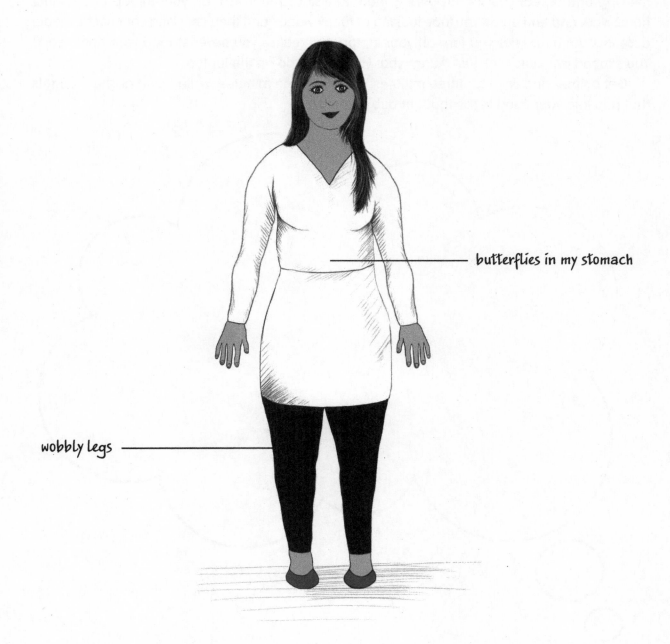

butterflies in my stomach

wobbly legs

Here and Now

Mindfulness helps us to pay attention to the here and now. This is actually something that we don't often do. Have you ever found yourself staring at the TV or your console screen, forgetting what you were doing as you were busy thinking about something else? This is an example of not being in the here and now but being in 'autopilot'. Autopilot is when you do things without thinking and repeat your behaviours without realising. You switch on your laptop to do some homework and end up on YouTube looking at funny videos and then checking your social media accounts. An hour later you turn off your laptop and realise you never started your homework! You slipped into autopilot, just doing what you always do on the laptop.

Get a timer and set it for three minutes. In these three minutes, write down all the thoughts that pop into your mind in the thought bubble below.

Wheel of Life

This exercise can be really useful if you feel things have become out of balance in your life, so perhaps you are spending too much time studying or revising and hardly any time with your family, or you are focused a lot on your friends and have little time for keeping yourself fit and healthy. The circle below represents your life; it is divided into sections to represent different parts of your life. If you wish, you can change the section headings to make them fit better for you or draw a new wheel.

On the circle below, show how much time and attention you give to the different parts of your life by colouring in the sections; for example, if you give a lot of attention to studying then colour the whole studying section in.

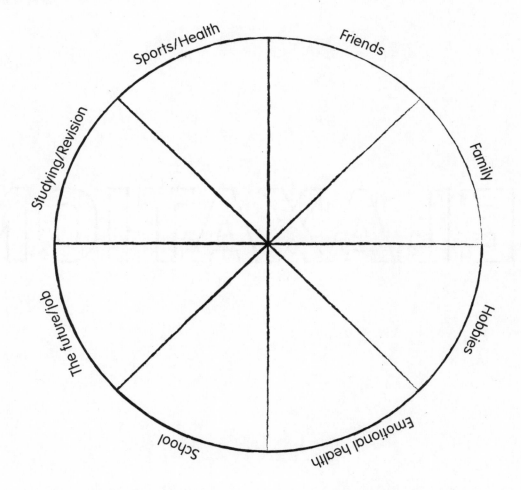

1. Review your wheel. Does the balance feel about right at the moment?

2. Which sections do you wish to pay more attention to?

3. What things could you do to help you get this new balance?

Colourful Relaxation

One method of keeping calm and relaxed is to spend some time colouring or doodling. The colouring or doodling allows you to switch off your brain from anxious thoughts and focus on the here and now. Let's try it out, by colouring in the word below and doodling around the page, perhaps drawing other words or things that make you feel relaxed. Don't rush this – take your time to make sure your brain has time to switch off.

Here and Now Five Senses Exercise

When you are worried or stressed about exams or tests it might seem tricky to be mindful and in the here and now. One exercise you can do to help you be present is to pay attention and notice your five senses.

The five senses to pay attention to are:

- hearing

- smell

- sight

- touch

- taste.

The first few times you do this exercise you might want to read the questions below but once you know what to do you can do this in your mind, so it's very easy to do when you are out and about.

1. **Hearing**
   Sit in silence and write down all the noises you can hear.

   _____

   _____

   _____

   _____

2. **Smell**
   Close your eyes. What can you smell?

   _____

   _____

   _____

   _____

3. Sight

What can you see around you, both near and far?

_____

_____

_____

_____

4. Touch

Notice what you feel touching you, your clothes or the furniture. Pay attention to which parts of you feel warmer or cooler.

_____

_____

_____

_____

5. Taste

What can you taste at the moment? There might be strong or faint tastes in your mouth.

_____

_____

_____

_____

Being Grateful for the Great Things!

When you have lots on your mind or when you are particularly stressed or worried it's easy to forget the good or great stuff. Try to find a moment each day to notice something that you are thankful or grateful for that day – it really can be anything. Have a go at this now; it can be harder than you think. Aiden has started his list of what he is grateful for in his life, so complete your list in the star over the page.

Family

Friend Amir

Rubik my dog

My maths skills

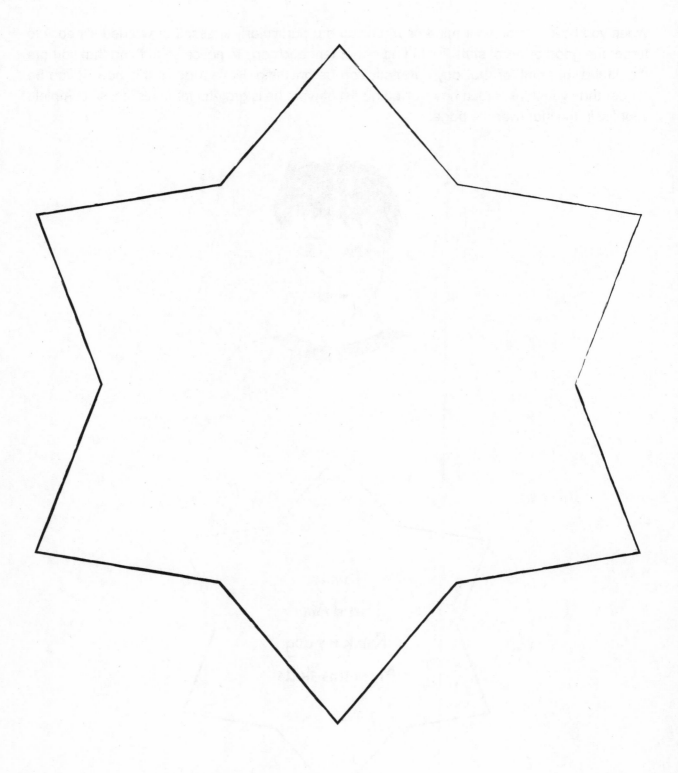

Awareness of Breath

Breathing is something you do automatically, without thinking about it, like your heart beating. Breathing just happens most of the time without you even noticing it.

For the next few seconds, focus on your breathing. Write below what you notice. What was your breathing like?

Often when we pay attention to our breathing it changes; it may become deeper or faster or slower.

There are many mindful breathing exercises available that encourage you to focus on your breathing without changing it. These exercises can help you feel calm and it can be helpful to practise them regularly. The idea is that by focusing on your breathing it takes you away from your other thoughts of 'I'm worried about…', 'If only I had…', 'I should have…', 'I must remember to…'. Even if these thoughts do pop into your head, it's okay, let them drift away and return your attention to your breathing.

If you search the internet for 'awareness of breath exercise for children', there will be lots of exercises to choose from. Pick some of the exercises and try them out; allow yourself to find one you like the best. Make a note of the exercises you try out and what you think of them over the page.

Name of exercise	Web address	How did I feel after the exercise?	Marks out of 10

Body Scan

Mindfulness practice can often involve a body scan exercise or meditation. This exercise will help you to focus your attention and take your mind away from your busy thoughts. This exercise can be practised every day or a few times a week. It will help you to work out where in your body you are feeling stressed and help you to release this stress from your body and mind.

Try to find somewhere quiet to carry out a body scan exercise, away from noise and other people, somewhere you won't be disturbed. The first few times you try this might feel a bit odd (and not very calming!). That's okay, just try and keep practising as it gets easier. As you practise the exercise a few times, you might not need to have the instructions.

You could ask someone to read out these instructions or you could record them onto your phone and play them back to yourself or you could look for a prepared body scan exercise on the internet.

1. **Get in position**
   Lie down on your back or sit somewhere comfortable. If you feel you can, try to close your eyes gently. Take a few moments to notice your breath and notice the movements in your body.

2. **Get comfortable and ready**
   Now take a minute to notice where your body makes contact with the chair or bed. As you breathe out, allow yourself to let go on each breath. We are going to focus our attention on each part of the body in turn.

3. **Notice your feet**
   Now focus your attention down your legs and to your feet. Focus on each of the toes on your foot in turn, notice each toe and what is touching each toe – it might be your socks, shoes or other toes or you might notice the space between your toes. What can you feel? You might feel tingling or maybe not really feel anything. It's okay, that's fine. Now move your awareness to the bottom of your feet, your heels and the rest of your feet, your ankles.

4. **Notice your legs**
   Shift your attention to the lower legs. What do you feel in your lower legs? Move up to the knee and then up to your thighs. Breathe in to your legs on the next in-breath and release on the out-breath. If your mind starts to wander, that's okay, turn your attention back to your legs.

5. **Notice your back and chest**
   Move up to your lower back and stomach area. Then move to your upper back and finally into your chest and shoulders. Breathe in to your back and stomach and then release on the out-breath. Be aware of how your chest expands as you breathe and then release. Try to notice your heart beating.

6. Notice your hands and arms

Gently shift your attention to your hands, fingers and thumbs. Notice each finger and what is touching it or the space between them. Notice any sensations in your fingers and then pay attention to the palms of your hands and the backs of your hands. Now focus on your wrists, lower arms, your elbows, your upper arms and then your shoulders and neck.

7. Notice your neck and head

Let your awareness slowly move up your neck and into your head and face. Try to relax your face on your next out-breath. Notice your jaw, your mouth and your lips and try to relax them. Now notice your nose, your cheeks, your ears, your eyes and your forehead.

8. Notice your whole body

Now try to be aware of your whole body. Feel your breath go in and out of your body from the tips of your toes to the top of your head.

9. Ending your body scan exercise

Now take a moment to congratulate yourself on making the time to do this exercise and look after yourself. Start to become aware of the world around you, any noises or sensations in the room. Gently wriggle your toes and begin to move your fingers. When you are ready, open your eyes and return your attention to the room.

What Could I Do If…?

Imagine yourself in the situations below, and think about how you might respond using the ideas you have learned from this chapter of the book.

Situation 1

You are sitting at your desk/table at home ready to start your homework or revision. You are finding it hard to get started, your mind is full of worries and stress. 'What if I don't get this finished tonight?', 'I wish I could be out with my friends having fun', 'I hate school work'. You notice your body feels very tense, you have a headache and your neck and shoulders are aching. What could you do to help settle your body and mind and be ready to start your work?

_____

_____

_____

_____

Situation 2

You are walking to school with your friends and you have a big test today; everyone is talking about the test. As you walk along, you feel a bit sick, you have butterflies in your stomach and wish you could turn around and go home and back to bed. What can you do to help yourself feel better and ready to take the test?

_____

_____

_____

_____

Mindfulness

Look back through the worksheets you have completed to help answer the questions below.

How does my body show that I am getting stressed?

_____

_____

_____

_____

What are my top three mindfulness exercises?

1. _____

2. _____

3. _____

Would doing mindfulness be a good area to work on?

Young person:	Yes ☐	No ☐	Maybe ☐
Adult:	Yes ☐	No ☐	Maybe ☐

If YES or MAYBE, see Chapter 10 for help with goal setting.

More on Mindfulness

Mindfulness is noticing your feelings, thoughts and body sensations in the present moment.

Have you ever had the experience of travelling in the car and arriving at your destination without noticing how you got there? Or perhaps of staring at the TV screen and realising you have missed some of what you are watching because you have zoned out? These are examples of not being aware or in the present moment.

These experiences of zoning out happen to us all, but all this thinking about the past or the future can lead to you feeling stressed out.

If you are able to practise mindfulness regularly it can have a number of positive effects, including:

- improved concentration

- being able to respond carefully to what you are feeling or thinking rather than being impulsive

- being more aware of your feelings, body sensations and thoughts.

A good first step to being in the present moment is to pay attention to your breathing. If you are focused and paying attention to your breathing, you are in the present moment. You are not thinking about yesterday or planning for tomorrow, but in the here and now.

You can use mindfulness in your daily life by bringing your awareness and noticing everyday tasks where you usually zone out, such as brushing your teeth, having a shower or walking to school.

Mindfulness practice can also involve longer, more formal exercises such as the body scan. Try out different ways of practising mindfulness and see what suits you.

MINDFULNESS: RESOURCES
Books

- *Sitting Still Like a Frog: Mindfulness Exercises for Kids* by Eline Snel, 2013, Shambhala.

- *No Worries: An Activity Book for Young People Who Sometimes Feel Anxious or Stressed* by Sharie Coombes, 2017, Studio Press.

- *Sane New World: Taming the Mind* by Ruby Wax, 2014, Hodder Paperbacks.

- *Cool Cats, Calm Kids: Relaxation and Stress Management for Young People* by Mary Williams and Dianne O'Quinn Burke, 2007, Impact Publishers.

- *The Stress Reduction Workbook for Teens*, second edition by Gina Biegel, 2017, Instant Help Books.

Websites

- www.mindfulnessinschools.org

- www.headspace.com

- www.smilingmind.com.au

- www.stopbreathethink.com

- www.buddhify.com

CHAPTER 7
The Big Day!

The focus of this chapter is on the actual day of the exam or test. It is important for the young person to be as calm as possible and not worried or distracted by other issues. It is useful to run through what will happen on the day in advance so that the young person can be prepared and nothing surprises them. This preparation time will also give them the opportunity to practise some of the suggested strategies in the correct setting. This advanced practising and rehearsal can be particularly important for young people with special educational needs.

This chapter will encourage the use of some of the strategies already explored and tried out in the rest of the book. It might be helpful to look through the worksheets previously completed to support thinking around on-the-day strategies.

OBJECTIVES

The worksheets in this chapter are designed to:

- help the young person reflect on previous experiences of being under pressure

- explore and try out strategies that can help when feeling under pressure

- enable the young person to identify what might be helpful on the day of an exam or test.

Under Pressure

Exams and tests can lead us to feel under pressure, stressed or anxious. I am certain you will have experienced these feelings at other times before, such as before a sports match or event, on your first day at a new school or before a school assembly or play. Have a think about a time in the past when you felt under pressure and use this example to fill in the worksheet below.

What under pressure challenge have you faced before?

_____

Spend some time thinking about how you coped with this. What did you do? What did you think? Did you get any extra help? How did you cope? Draw or write about that time below:

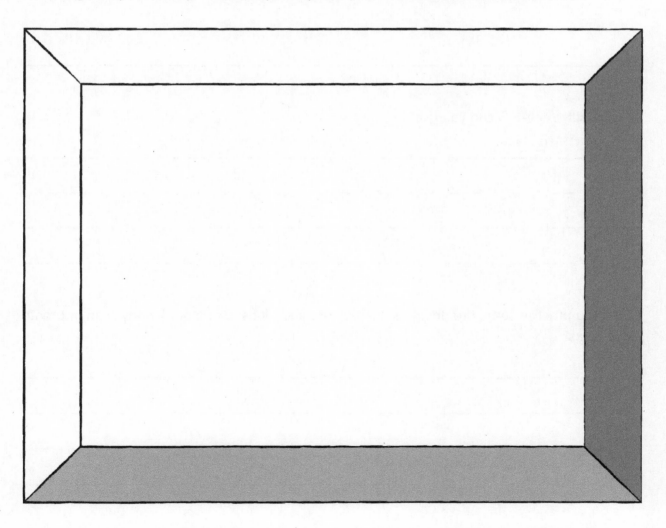

Have a good look at the things that helped you get through this time. They might be things that you can do the next time you feel under pressure!

Waiting to Go In

Often those ten minutes or so before you go into an exam can be very stressful. You are waiting outside the room with your friends, some are telling you about their revision, some are still revising, and others tell you that they don't care about the exam anyway! Let's think together about the best way to manage this waiting.

Who do you want to spend this time with? Do you think certain people will help you to keep calm or make you more stressed? Would it be best to be with others or on your own?

_____

_____

_____

_____

What positive self-talk can you use?

_____

_____

_____

_____

Could you practise some breathing techniques or mindfulness like a quick body scan or breath awareness?

_____

_____

_____

_____

Would you prefer to have headphones in to block out the conversations of those around you?

_____

_____

_____

_____

What else would you find helpful to do while you are waiting?

_____

_____

_____

_____

In the Exam Room

It can feel strange and different in the exam room, particularly the first few times you take exams. It is good to be prepared for what to expect, which is why many schools give students the chance to take practice papers or mocks. If you are particularly worried, you might want to ask if you can look around the exam room before the day itself to get used to it. Have a think about these situations below, so you are ready for anything! Write down what you think you should do. If you get stuck, ask an adult for their ideas.

You read the first few questions and feel as if you have forgotten everything and don't know what to write.

_____

_____

_____

_____

The person seated next to you tries to talk to you during the exam.

_____

_____

_____

_____

You feel sick and think you need to leave the room.

_____

_____

_____

_____

There is severe weather and you get stuck travelling to school and think you might be late.

_____

_____

_____

_____

Planning Checklist

It can be useful to think through in advance what will be happening on the day of your test or exam, as this will stop you worrying about the little details. Some people also find it helpful to have a checklist of the practical things they need to remember – this allows you to put things on the checklist and reduce your worry. Fill in the planning checklist below and add anything extra you can think of – then all you will have to remember is the checklist!

Checklist

1. What I will have for breakfast? _____
2. Where is the exam or test happening? _____
3. How am I getting there? _____
4. What time does the exam start? _____
5. What time do I need to leave? _____
6. What equipment do I need (pens/pencils)? _____
7. Have I packed my equipment? _____
8. Have I packed some tissues and a bottle of water? _____
9. _____
10. _____

Mindful Word Search

Twelve words linked with mindfulness are hidden in the grid below. Word searches can be a really good way of being in the moment, as you are so busy searching for the words your brain doesn't have time for worries. You could try doing a word search on the day of an exam or test to help you practise being mindful. Check your answers using the answer sheet in the 'Top Tips for Young People' at the end of this chapter.

R	O	L	R	T	N	E	M	O	M
A	C	C	E	P	T	S	T	V	L
X	B	B	L	D	F	O	E	H	A
A	S	R	A	T	U	C	I	F	C
L	N	E	X	F	O	C	U	S	B
G	O	A	L	S	M	P	Q	E	K
A	T	T	E	N	T	I	O	N	H
Y	I	H	I	P	M	I	F	S	R
T	C	A	C	J	K	C	L	E	P
X	E	S	O	U	N	D	N	L	M

Words to search for:

ACCEPT	NOTICE
ATTENTION	QUIET
BREATH	RELAX
CALM	SENSE
FOCUS	SOUND
MOMENT	STILL

Mindful Tests or Exams

Chapter 6 focused on developing your skills in mindfulness, and you can use these skills when taking an exam or test. It is important to practise these skills before taking the test or exam, so perhaps try with a piece of homework or set up a practice test.

1. Make sure you are sitting comfortably.

2. Place your hands loosely on the desk or in your lap.

3. Notice what sounds you can hear around you; allow yourself to be in the moment, in the room.

4. Start to notice your breathing – remember not to change it, just notice and pay attention to each breath you take.

5. Complete a brief body scan, noticing how your body feels from your toes to the top of your head.

6. If you notice you are feeling worried or stressed, take a deep breath. Slowly breathe out and as you do, imagine that you are breathing out the stress and worry.

7. Take another deep breath if you feel you need to.

8. Return to your normal breathing; imagine doing your homework or taking your test calmly and confidently.

9. Gently begin to move. You are now ready to start your homework or test.

Did you notice anything different when you did this mindful exercise before your homework or test?

_____

_____

_____

_____

_____

_____

Finished!

Looking after yourself when you have finished an exam or test is just as important as the preparation beforehand. At times you may have more than one exam in a day and so staying calm is crucial so you are ready for the next one!

The following thoughts might pop into your head when you have finished. Colour in those that apply to you and add some of your own.

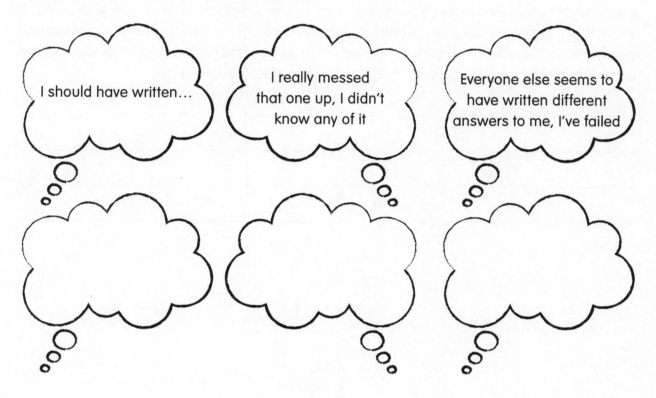

Now try and write some more realistic thoughts that will help you to feel calm.

What Could I Do If...?

Imagine yourself in the situations below and think about how you might respond, using the ideas you have learned from this chapter of the book.

Situation 1

It's the night before your big maths exam and you are messaging your friends on your phone. It sounds as if they have done loads more revision than you. You begin to feel very stressed and worried about tomorrow. You think to yourself, 'I am going to fail this exam', 'I have always been rubbish at maths' and 'My parents are going to be so disappointed in me.'

_____

_____

_____

_____

Situation 2

You have just finished your history exam and you are feeling pretty upset and annoyed. The exam was really difficult and for some questions you didn't even write an answer. You are walking home now and trying hard not to cry. You have a science exam later, after lunch. What could you do?

_____

_____

_____

_____

The Big Day!

Look back through the worksheets you have completed to help answer the questions below.

What are some important things about:

- the times when you manage okay when feeling under pressure?

_____

_____

_____

- the times when you struggle when feeling under pressure?

_____

_____

_____

What are my top three strategies for coping with stress and anxiety on the day of an exam?

1. _____

2. _____

3. _____

Would doing staying calm on exam day be a good area to work on?

Young person:	Yes ☐	No ☐	Maybe ☐
Adult:	Yes ☐	No ☐	Maybe ☐

If YES or MAYBE, see Chapter 10 for help with goal setting.

The Big Day!

Here are some extra tips on taking exams or tests:

- Breathe slowly and deeply while waiting for the exam to start.

- Before starting the exam, read the instructions.

- If you are unsure about the instructions, ask the teacher.

- Before starting writing, read all the questions and make sure you know how many questions you have to answer – perhaps even plan how much time to spend on each question.

- You could start by answering the question you feel you can answer best.

- If you get stuck on a question, try the next one. You can always come back to it later. If you are really stuck, try to have a guess anyway.

- Try to leave time to read through and check your answers before the exam finishes.

MINDFUL WORD SEARCH ANSWER SHEET

Did you find all the answers? Did it help you be in the moment?

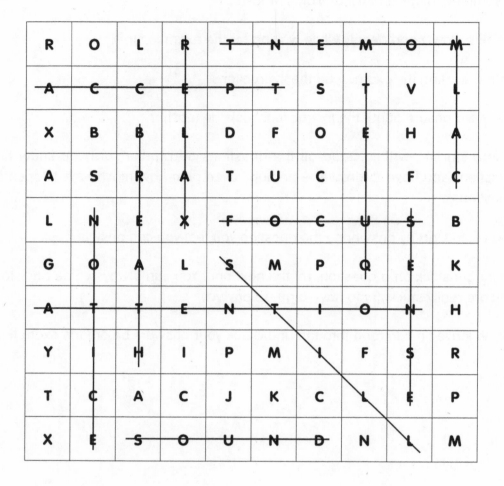

CHAPTER 8

Special Educational Needs and Exams

Exams and tests can be stressful and difficult for many people, but even more so for those children and young people who have special educational needs (SEN). This chapter is dedicated to supporting children and young people with a broad range of SEN. Some may have their needs identified through a diagnosis such as learning disability, autism spectrum condition, attention deficit hyperactivity disorder (ADHD), dyslexia, dyscalculia or dyspraxia. Others may have identified needs but no diagnosis. Some of the children may have an education, health and care plan (EHCP) or be placed on the SEN Register for their school, and others may not.

Many children and young people who have SEN will meet the criteria for special access arrangements for their exams, which are designed to go some way towards mitigating their difficulties. The exams regulator updates the guidance regularly as to what are identified difficulties and the effect these have on students who are considered eligible. It is important to consider access arrangements as early as possible in order to make the applications and give students the chance to take practice tests with adjustments in place.

All of the chapters in this book are beneficial to those with SEN, but this chapter allows some additional thought and reflection for those students and the adults supporting them.

OBJECTIVES

The worksheets in this chapter are designed to:

- help the young person to further consider their revision planning, particularly considering their individual learning profile, strengths and needs.

- help the young person identify and try out additional strategies that are effective in supporting them during study and exams.

Revision Planning Quiz

All students learn differently and it is essential to plan revision sessions so that they take advantage of your strengths. When you are revising, it is important to feel comfortable, be able to concentrate and be able to learn what you are working on. Fill in the quiz below to find out what is important to you for revision. Circle the answer that applies to you.

1. What time of day do you prefer to study?

    Morning   Afternoon   Evening

2. Do you like to study on your own or with friends?

    On my own   With one other person   In a group

3. Where do you prefer to study?

    In my bedroom   In the lounge/dining room   In a cafe   In the library

4. How long do you like to study before taking a break?

    20 minutes   30 minutes   45 minutes   1 hour

5. How do you prefer to study?

    Make notes   Draw mind maps   Take practice papers   Discuss learning

Memory Skills

Memory is a skill that can be improved with practice, just like kicking a football, riding a bike or drawing a picture. Memory skills can help us during tests and exams as we often have to try and remember what we have already learned in lessons. This worksheet will encourage you to consider your memory skills and give you some ideas on how to practise them.

Let's challenge your memory with some fun games!

Missing item challenge: Ten everyday items are placed on a tray (key, coin, pen, marble, string etc.) and players are allowed to look at the tray for one minute. Then the tray is covered, one item is secretly taken away, and the tray is revealed again. Players must guess which item is missing.

I'm going on holiday: The game starts with one player saying, 'I'm going on holiday. I am packing my suitcase and I am taking with me…'. The next person then repeats the phrase and adds another item. This continues with each player saying the phrase, all the other items and adding their own. If a player makes a mistake they are out of the round.

Backwards!: Spell your name backwards or say the alphabet backwards!

Coin game: Five coins are placed in a sequence on the table and players are allowed to look at the sequence. Next, the coins are covered and players have to replicate the sequence from their own pile of coins. They are timed to see how long it takes them. The winner is the player with the fastest time and best accuracy. The number of coins can be increased to make the challenge more difficult!

Category quiz: Players need to list words that fit in a particular category in a set amount of time; for example, list all the breeds of dog you know, list all the kings and queens of England you know, list all the Shakespeare plays you can remember.

Many board and card games also use memory skills, so you could have a go with a game!

Revision Timetable

Schools sometimes give all their students study leave during exams. This means that you don't have to go to school at the usual times and instead have to just go in for your exams. The time you are not at school should be used to study and revise for your exams. This change to routine and more unstructured time can be difficult for some people. It can be helpful to create a revision timetable to help you plan which subjects to revise when, and to make sure you build in time for exercise, relaxation and having fun! Use the timetable below to help you plan your week.

Day	Morning (9am–12)	Afternoon (12–5pm)	Evening (5–9pm)
Monday			
Tuesday			
Wednesday			
Thursday			
Friday			
Saturday			
Sunday			

Mind Maps

Mind mapping is a technique you can use as part of your revision that will help you organise your thinking and help you recall the information you want during your exams. Mind maps save you writing lots of notes as you can create a map for a subject or topic that includes words, figures and images.

TIPS

- Start with a central image or word to represent the subject or topic.

- Add in main branches from the central idea – the branches can represent the key facts and figures that you need to remember.

- Add in further smaller branches with more detailed information or ideas.

- Make connections between branches.

- Notice where the gaps are on your map – you probably need to focus your revision on these areas.

Create a mind map below on a topic of your choice. It could be your favourite subject at school, a hobby or interest or even your pet. This is just a chance to practise this technique.

Movement Breaks

Sometimes we need to give our brains extra stimulation to keep ourselves focused. By moving our body and working our muscles, we can help to keep our mind alert and organised. Some movements work better than others, so good tips to remember are *maintain a steady pace, make it hard* and *keep going.* Try the exercises below and rate them by colouring in or circling the number of stars you think they deserve. Rate them on how fun they are and how effective they are at keeping you focused. You will need to work out with an adult which of these exercises you could use in a test or exam and which might be better to try when you are revising. It might partly depend on whether you are taking your exams in a small side room or in a large exam hall.

Exercises you can do at your desk

Exercise	How to	Star rating
Chair push-ups	Put your hands on the sides of the chair seat and push down so that you lift your bottom off the chair. Make sure your feet are off the floor! Do 10–20.	Fun: ☆ ☆ ☆ ☆ ☆ Effective: ☆ ☆ ☆ ☆ ☆
Hand presses	Place your palms together and press them against each other as hard as you can. Hold for ten seconds, repeat five times.	Fun: ☆ ☆ ☆ ☆ ☆ Effective: ☆ ☆ ☆ ☆ ☆
Head presses	First sit up straight. Link your fingers together and place your hands on top of your head, then push down firmly. Hold for ten seconds, repeat five times.	Fun: ☆ ☆ ☆ ☆ ☆ Effective: ☆ ☆ ☆ ☆ ☆
Sports water bottle	Have a drink from a bottle with a sports top that takes a lot of effort to suck through.	Fun: ☆ ☆ ☆ ☆ ☆ Effective: ☆ ☆ ☆ ☆ ☆

Exercises you can do with a bit of space

Exercise	How to	Star rating
Wall or floor push-ups	Try push-ups standing against the wall or on the floor. Make sure your hands are under your shoulders and you bend and straighten your arms and keep your body still! Do 15–20.	Fun: ☆ ☆ ☆ ☆ ☆ Effective: ☆ ☆ ☆ ☆ ☆
Handstand against the wall	Start on your hands and knees and then 'walk' your feet up the wall behind you until your body is straight. Keep your feet leaning on the wall and hold for 15–20 seconds.	Fun: ☆ ☆ ☆ ☆ ☆ Effective: ☆ ☆ ☆ ☆ ☆
Table top	Sit on the floor, lean back and push your middle up so that your hands and feet are on the ground and your body and thighs are straight like a 'table top'. Hold for 20 seconds.	Fun: ☆ ☆ ☆ ☆ ☆ Effective: ☆ ☆ ☆ ☆ ☆

Exercises that also 'help out'. Can you think of any others? Add to the table above.

Pushing/pulling heavy equipment (e.g. sports gear)	Walking with a heavy backpack
Using a hand or foot pump to inflate balls/tyres	Crushing cans for recycling
Pushing a lawn mower/wheelbarrow/vacuum	Digging in the garden
Carrying heavy loads (e.g. book box)	Stacking/unstacking chairs

SEN and Exams

Look back through the worksheets you have completed to help you answer the questions below:

Are there any strategies from this chapter that you think will help with your exams?

Yes   No

What strategies will you try and use from this chapter?

_____

_____

_____

_____

_____

_____

_____

Access Arrangements

Schools, parents, carers and young people should consider, together with the support of professional experts such as educational psychologists, whether a young person's needs may make them eligible for access arrangements to be put in place. Evidence that may support this could include:

- Frequently making spelling or grammatical errors.

- Reading a passage but being unable to answer questions about it.

- Experiencing pain when writing for significant periods of time.

- Struggling with reading/slow reading.

- Finding that words move around the page or seem blurred.

- Unable to sustain concentration for sustained periods of time.

- Unable to remain seated for the length of an exam.

- Running out of time to copy work off the board.

- Writing slowly or in an untidy way.

- Unable to keep up with taking notes.

- Getting 'stuck' and unable to move on.

- Having problems getting ideas down on paper, despite doing an essay plan.

- Having problems reading questions and thinking aloud.

It is important to be aware of what possible reasonable adjustments or access arrangements can be put into place. They may include one or more of the following:

- additional time

- reader (human or computer)

- word processor

- scribe

- prompter

- practical assistant

- enlarged papers

- modified paper (colour, font size, braille, language etc.)

- smaller/individual room

- rest breaks.

It is important that the adjustments are appropriate to the exam and individual student; for example, during a practical exam a student with dyslexia may not require additional time but during a written exam they would do.

SEN AND EXAMS: RESOURCES
Books

- *Helping Kids and Teens with ADHD in School: A Workbook for Classroom Support and Managing Transitions* by Joanne Steer and Kate Horstmann, 2009, Jessica Kingsley Publishers.

- *All Birds Have Anxiety* by Kathy Hoopman, 2017, Jessica Kingsley Publishers.

- *Asperger's Syndrome and Anxiety: by the girl with the curly hair*, volume 8 by Alis Rowe, 2014, Lonely Mind Books.

- *The Incredible 5 Point Scale: The Significantly Improved and Expanded Second Edition* by Kari Dunn Buron and Mitzi Curtis, 2012, AAPC Publishing.

- *The Self-Help Guide for Teens with Dyslexia* by Alais Winton, 2015, Jessica Kingsley Publishers.

- *Mind Maps for Kids: Study Skills* by Tony Buzan, 2008, Harper Thorsons.

Websites

- www.specialneedsjungle.com
- www.jcq.org.uk/exams-office/access-arrangements-and-special-consideration
- www.getrevising.co.uk

CHAPTER 9

Family Support

The concept of family is a diverse one, so in order to keep it simple I will use the term parents, but this will mean different things to different people. A parent could be a mother, father, step-parent, grandparent, foster carer, adoptive parent, aunt, uncle, brother, sister or friend.

Exam time can be a time of stress for children and young people but also for the whole family. Parents want their children to do their best and can worry about what will happen if they don't get their expected results. An understanding family can be very beneficial during tests and exams. Having adults who are available, encouraging, ready to talk about feelings, supportive of rest time and the balance between study and relaxation will really help.

It is important to give a balanced message to children and young people about the importance of exams, not only during exam season but throughout their lives. Often unintentionally, families can add to the pressure to succeed and do well. Families can face the challenge of a child who seems to do very little revision, appears unmotivated and not to care about their exams. In contrast, other families are faced with a child who never stops revising and is too focused on doing well.

OBJECTIVES

The worksheets and advice sheets in this chapter are designed to:

- help the young person and their family develop positive support strategies around exam stress

- help parents and other supportive adults consider what messages they are giving children and young people about tests, exams and academic performance.

Leave Me Alone

Parents often want to be encouraging and supportive during revision or before an exam or test. However, what can happen is misunderstandings, arguments, slammed doors and storming off. Here are some examples of things parents say which young people don't find helpful – add any more you can think of. Then consider what would be helpful for you to hear from a parent or supportive adult.

Not helpful

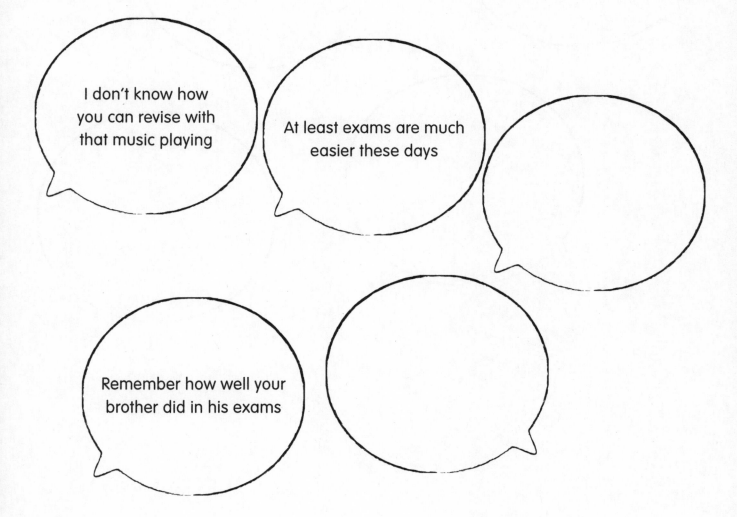

Helpful

Family Survey

Photocopy or download this worksheet and give it to members of your family/the people that you live with. Ask everyone to complete the survey on their own. Arrange a family meeting where you can all sit down together and talk about your answers. No one is allowed to get angry or upset. Listen to each other and try to understand each other's points of view.

Who in this family gets stressed or worried? What do they get stressed or worried about?

_____

_____

_____

Who notices first that they are stressed or worried? What do they notice?

_____

_____

_____

Who in this family stays calm?

_____

_____

_____

How does everyone else in the family respond to their calmness?

_____

_____

_____

For every member of the family (including yourself) identify one strength.

_____

_____

_____

Family Stories

Over time, stories take shape in families about all sorts of different subjects; for example, in our family we always stand up for what we believe, or in our family we work hard to get where we are, or in our family the men/boys are useless at maths, or in our family the women/girls always have messy handwriting.

In your family, what stories are there about the following areas? If you don't know, ask other members of your family to see what they say.

School

_____

_____

_____

Exams

_____

_____

_____

University

_____

_____

_____

Getting a job

_____

_____

_____

Maths

_____

_____

_____

Art

_____

_____

_____

Success

_____

_____

_____

English literature

_____

_____

_____

Advance Communication

Exam time can be a stressful for the whole family, so arguments can break out over the smallest things as everyone is feeling a little bit snappy. It's a good idea to talk to your parents about what they can do to support you during the exams in advance. Have a go at filling in this worksheet by circling the answers that apply to you. Then take some time to sit down with a parent or supportive adult and talk through your answers.

1. When you are revising for a test or exam, how would you like your parent to support you?

    Leave me alone   Bring me a drink/snack

    Test me on what I have learned   Sit with me sometimes

2. On the morning of your test or exam, how would you like your parent to support you?

    Leave me alone   Make my breakfast   Give me a lift to school

    Give me a quick test   Check I have everything I need   Wish me luck

    Talk to me about other things   Do a mindfulness exercise with me

    Remind me of positive self-talk

3. After a test or exam, how would you like your parent to support you?

    Leave me alone   Ask me how I did   Talk to me about other things

    Make my favourite dinner   Do a mindfulness exercise with me

Mindful Parenting

Parenting is one of the hardest jobs in the world and there is so much advice and opinion on how to do it 'right'. If you want to try and bring mindfulness into your parenting, then try to do so in a non-judgemental and low-pressure way. A mindful parent is a parent who brings awareness to what they are doing, a parent who can pause and a parent who feels connected to how they are feeling in themselves and how their children are feeling.

You may live a busy life and respond and react automatically, saying and doing the things you always say and do. This might mean you are angry or irritated with your children, perhaps raising your voice at times. In order to slow down our responses and try different ways of thinking, we need to develop our pause button. The pause button will give you a breather, and this breathing space will be just long enough to stop you reacting automatically and allow your rational mind to respond.

Next time you find yourself in an overwhelming or stressful situation:

STOP
BREATHE
NOTICE
REFLECT
RESPOND

Developing your pause button could be something you do as a whole family. If everyone is stopping and taking a breath, the positive effects will be magnified and family life could begin to feel very different.

Compliments: The Family Challenge

Sometimes we are so busy rushing around with work, hobbies and school that we forget to tell the important people in our lives when they do something well or when they are helpful, kind or fun. This is particularly important at times of stress such as exam time, when often tensions can run high in the whole family. So ask your family if they will take on this 'family challenge' over the next week. Each person has to give everyone else in the family two compliments a day. For example, you might say to your mum or dad, 'Thanks for my dinner, it tasted delicious', or to your sister or brother, 'Thanks for getting my knife and fork; it was kind of you.'

A good rule when giving someone a compliment is to try and include two parts:

What they did +	**Why it was good** =	**The perfect compliment!**

Some examples are:

What they did	Why it was good	The perfect compliment!
'Thanks for…getting me a drink/letting me choose the channel/helping with my work/listening to me.'	'It was really…kind/ thoughtful/hard working/generous/ funny/friendly/fun.'	'Thanks for giving the family challenge a go and finding good things to say about everyone. It was really impressive!'

Put a copy of this on the fridge to remind everyone – copy it onto bright paper so it stands out!

At the end of the week, fill in the table on the next page to see how everyone got on with the family challenge. Remember to give compliments for trying.

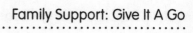

The family challenge: how did we go?

Name of family member	Example of a compliment given (and who they gave it to)	Did they pass the challenge?	Did they like the challenge?

Family Support

Look back through the worksheets you have completed to help answer the questions below.

How do we support each other well in my family?

_____

_____

_____

_____

How can we improve support for each other in my family?

_____

_____

_____

_____

Would support in my family be a good area to work on?

Young person:	Yes ☐	No ☐	Maybe ☐
Adult:	Yes ☐	No ☐	Maybe ☐

If YES or MAYBE, see Chapter 10 for help with goal setting.

Revision Support

Every child and young person is different and you will know your child best of all, but here are some general ideas which might be helpful to you.

- Make sure they have a comfortable place to study which is quiet and away from busy family life.

- If there is no suitable study spot at home, perhaps they could revise at a friend's house or the library. If they are old enough to be left at home, it might be easier if you leave them alone at home for a short time.

- If your child finds it easier to concentrate with background music or noise then allow them to do so.

- Support your child to develop a revision timetable and try to work with this where you can.

- Try to avoid nagging them about revision.

- Where possible, relieve them of other family chores and jobs.

- Try to be understanding of their stress and worry, which on the outside might look more like anger, grumpiness or rudeness.

- Encourage regular breaks.

- If you are able to, reward them for the effort they are putting into study and revision.

- Try to remain calm yourself, do not pile on the pressure, but instead keep things in perspective.

FAMILY SUPPORT: RESOURCES
Books

- *Five Deep Breaths: The Power of Mindful Parenting* by Genevieve von Lob, 2017, Bantam Press.

- *Overcoming Your Child's Fears and Worries: A Self-Help Guide Using Cognitive Behavioural Techniques* by Cathy Cresswell and Lucy Willetts, 2007, Robinson.

- *Parenting Your Anxious Child with Mindfulness and Acceptance: A Powerful New Approach to Overcoming Fear, Panic, and Worry Using Acceptance and Commitment Therapy* by Christopher McCurry, 2009, New Harbinger.

Websites

- www.familylives.org.uk
- www.familiesonline.co.uk

CHAPTER 10

The Future and Beyond

The aim of this final chapter is to help you pull together all the detections, reflections and strategies you have discovered while working through the book and move them into a plan for the future and beyond. It will also give you and the young person a chance to reflect on your experiences, and to celebrate your hard work and successes.

In each completed chapter, you have identified those areas thought to be in need of further development and focused support (the 'Pulling It Together' pages). Now is the time to:

- prioritise these areas

- create specific goals and action plans

- put things into action

- make real and lasting changes.

Select only one or two skills to work on at a time to help focus your energy. Some people have found that by sharing decisions, the young person's motivation and sense of ownership can be significantly increased (e.g. the young person chooses one skill and the adult the other). Try strategies for at least four weeks in order to ensure adequate practice to turn them into habits. Once successfully implemented, these strategies will become part of daily life and you will be able to choose new goals to work towards. It is also important to recognise that priorities change over time, and you may need to revisit a section of the book at a later date.

From experience, I have learned that in creating and working towards change there are some key elements to success. Some useful considerations are listed in the 'Top Tips' section. The principles for success include:

1. Choose goals that are valued by those involved, so that everyone is motivated to achieve the outcome. Work towards having a clear but realistic 'picture' of what life would be like if the goal was achieved and the benefits it would have. Try and keep that image in your mind!

2. Recognise that achieving goals will require additional resources and involve changes for all. A commitment of time and energy will be needed for success, especially when people need to change their behaviour. If you can't commit adequate time, then perhaps don't set the goals! Otherwise you will only be setting yourself and the young person up for failure.

3. Celebrate both effort and success! This is vital in sustaining the process of growth and learning. You may need to use rewards and motivators to provide the energy and motivation to continue. Remember that these celebrations are not just for the young person – the adults working with them need to share the triumph!

4. Make working towards goals part of daily life.

5. Remember that effective goal setting is a crucial element that needs thoughtful and careful planning. In recognition of this, the goal-setting sheets in this chapter are designed to help support a SMART process. Good goal setting does not happen on its own, even for those with lots of experience. How many times have you set yourself a general goal such as 'get fit'? How much better would it be to set yourself a 'SMARTer' goal such as 'Sign up to the sports centre and go twice a week for a month'? So what are 'SMART' goals and how do you set them?

Specific   Make goals specific so that they answer the six 'W' questions: who, what, where, when, which and why.

Measurable   Set definite criteria so progress can be measured – how much, how many and so on. This ensures that everyone will know when the goal has been achieved.

Attainable   Set small, achievable goals, even if you have to set a number of smaller steps before achieving a larger goal. Consider what is attainable in light of your timeframe (see below).

Realistic   Use your knowledge of the young person's skills and their environment and determine what is realistic. Be aware that goals that include concepts such as 'always' and '100 per cent' may never be achievable.

Timely   Set a clear timeframe in which to achieve the goal. A shorter timeframe will be more effective in keeping everyone on track and energised.

When it comes to setting goals based on the work you have completed in this book, there are many different formats you can use. Do try to keep the SMART principles in mind and address the practical considerations outlined in the goal-setting worksheets included later in this chapter. There is also an accompanying goal review sheet included to help facilitate the second stage of the process.

Before you start your last series of 'Detect and Reflect', 'Give It A Go', 'Pulling It Together' and 'Top Tips', I would like to say CONGRATULATIONS! Your increased understanding and empathy of exam stress will go a long way and make a real difference for these young people. I hope you continue to enjoy the journey!

The Best Bits (Young Person)

Take a few moments to think about the work you have completed so far in this book. Have a flick through all the sheets you have done – that is *a lot* of work! In the shapes below, draw or write some of the things you have found the most fun, the most useful and the most interesting. It is important that the adult you have been working with does this as well, so there is a worksheet for them to do at the same time on the next page.

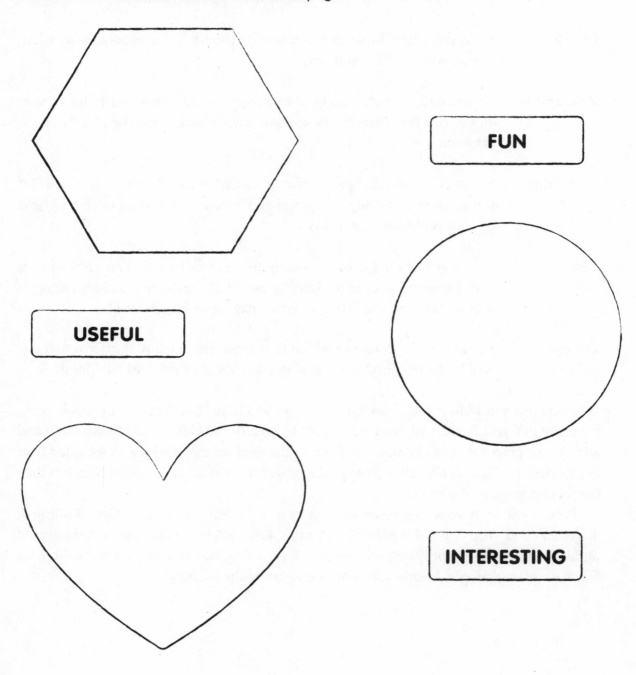

sss

The Best Bits (Adults)

Look back through your own folder and reflections sheets and think about all the work completed by you and the young person during the course of this book. Draw or write about what you found the most fun, the most useful and the most interesting in the shapes below. Compare your answers with each other's!

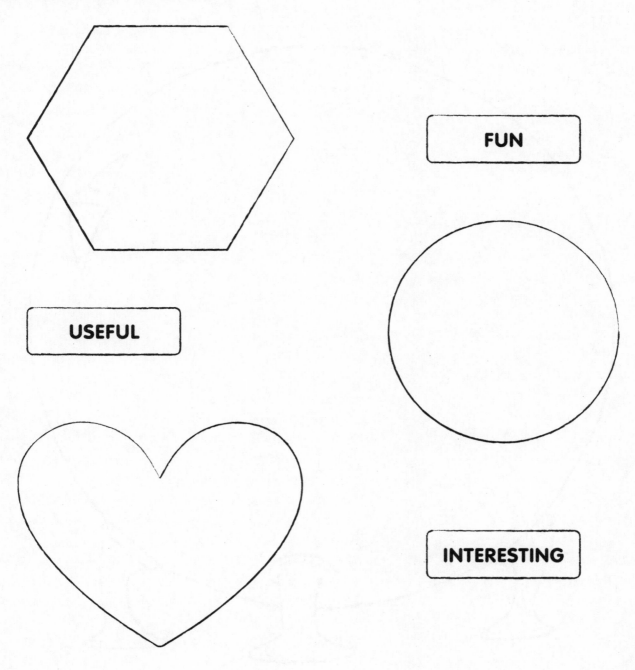

FUN

USEFUL

INTERESTING

Looking into a Crystal Ball

Imagine you have a crystal ball and you can see two years into the future. What will your life be like? How will you be getting on in school/college/university? What activities or hobbies do you hope to be doing? What will be happening in your family? Draw or write some of your predictions in the crystal ball below.

Identifying Goals

Now comes the fun part – putting ideas into action! Fill out the mind map on the next page to help work out which goals to work on, and in what order. Work through the following steps:

1. Look back through all the 'Pulling It Together' sheets at the end of each chapter. For those that you have identified as an area to 'work on', write the name of the chapter into the circles in the mind map. If you can, write each one in a different colour. If you need to add more circles, draw them in or draw your own mind map on a big sheet of paper.

2. From each circle, draw other lines and circles and write down important things from that particular chapter. These are the ideas that might help you figure out your goals, such as specific things you find difficult and strategies you thought might work well.

3. Once this is done, choose the top three things that you would like to work on and highlight them. This could be a general skill area (e.g. mindfulness) or a particular strategy (e.g. positive thinking). Then ask your adult to highlight their top three in another colour.

4. Compare your top three goals and agree on one or two to start off with. These will become your goals.

5. Read through the example goal sheets that Lily and Aiden have filled out. These will give you some ideas on how to complete yours.

6. Remember to keep your mind map because after you have achieved the first few goals, you can come back and pick out a few more!

Identifying Goals: Mind Map

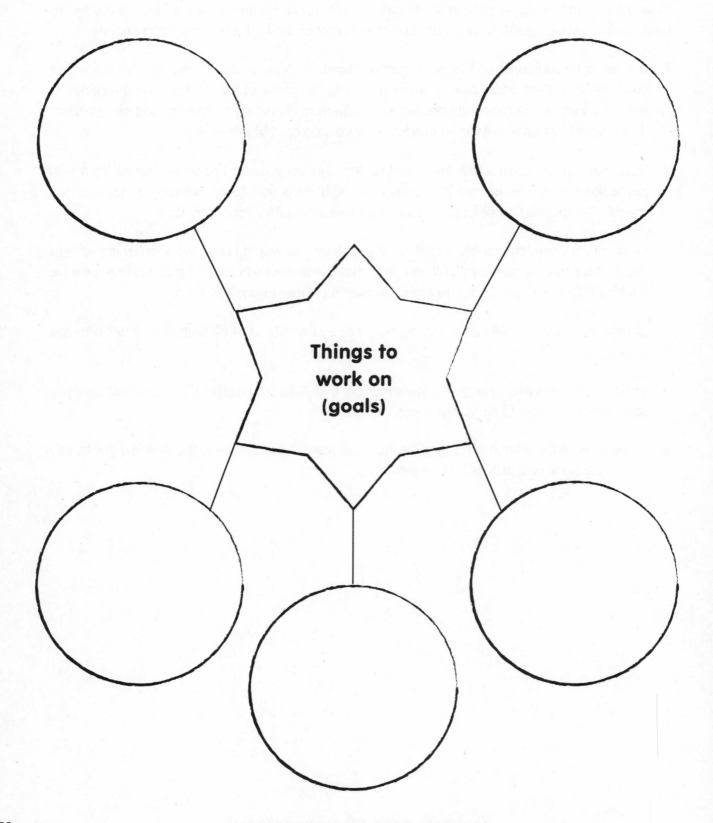

Goal Setting

Lily has completed the sheet below and has shown her form teacher – have a look at her ideas.

Goal setting for: Lily	Date: November
General aim	Gain a better balance between study and relaxation
SMART goal (Specific, Measurable, Attainable, Realistic, Timely)	To spend at least 1 hour every evening relaxing and not studying
What strategies will be used?	Regular exercise More breaks
Who will do what?	Lily to create schedule Mum to pay for swimming
How will we know if it's working and how will you measure this?	Feel less stressed More time spent relaxing/not studying
When to check progress	1 week
What is the small reward if the goal is achieved?	Trip to the cinema

Aiden has agreed a goal to work on with his mum and teaching assistant and completed the worksheet below.

Goal setting for: Aiden	Date: April
General aim	To feel less worried about exams
SMART goal (Specific, Measurable, Attainable, Realistic, Timely)	To be 4/10 calm before the next exam I do
What strategies will be used?	Positive self-talk Awareness of breath exercise
Who will do what?	Practise awareness of breath exercise with Mum four times a week Teaching assistant to print out positive self-talk reminder cards
How will we know if it's working and how will you measure this?	Anxiety rating will reduce Measure with scaling, e.g. give worry a mark out of 10 (10 = very worried)
When to check progress	3 weeks
What is the small reward if the goal is achieved?	New console magazine

Goal-Setting Sheet

Goal setting for:	Date:
General aim	
SMART goal (Specific, Measurable, Attainable, Realistic, Timely)	
What strategies will be used?	
Who will do what?	
How will we know if it's working and how will you measure this?	
When to check progress	
What is the small reward if the goal is achieved?	

Goal Review Sheet

Goal review for:	Date:
SMART goal	
Was the goal met?	
Was the plan fully put in place?	
Which strategies helped?	
Which strategies didn't help?	
Reward to be given	

Reflect on the above and decide on one of the following actions:

Goal not met: keep working on revised goal	Review the original goal-setting sheet and the information above – what changes are needed?
Goal met: consider how to continue with the strategies	Agree systems for ongoing monitoring and rewards. Consider what level of adult support might be required.

Congratulations!

The certificate on the next page is to congratulate you on all the hard work you have undertaken, so please fill it in and decorate it. You could also make another one for the adult who has helped you in working through this book! There are blank spaces so that all of your great achievements can be celebrated; this could be creativity, calmness, energy or hard work. Try photocopying the certificate onto coloured paper if you want to make it really stand out!

You might also want to celebrate all your hard work and achievements in another way. Perhaps you could go out for an ice cream, a picnic at the park or if you are part of an exam stress group, have a little party!

CERTIFICATE OF EXCELLENCE

This award goes to:

For:

Signed:

Date:

APPENDIX

Pictures of Oliver, Lily and Aiden

OLIVER

LILY

AIDEN